LUTHERAN-ROMAN CATHOLIC JOINT COMMISSION

CHURCH AND JUSTIFICATION

UNDERSTANDING THE CHURCH IN THE LIGHT OF THE DOCTRINE OF JUSTIFICATION

Published by
The Lutheran World Federation
1994

Translated from the Original German Text

KIRCHE UND RECHTFERTIGUNG

(Verlag Bonifatius-Druckerei Paderborn/Verlag Otto Lembeck
Frankfurt am Main, 1994)

ISBN 3-906706-14-1

(ISBN 3-87088-828-8 Verlag Bonifatius — German Edition)
(ISBN 3-87476-299-8 Verlag Lembeck — German Edition)

CONTENTS

Foreword 7

Abbreviations 11

1. **Justification and the Church** 13

   1.1 Justification and the Church as Truths of Faith 14

   1.2 Justification and the Church Founded in the Mystery of Christ and of the Trinity 15

   1.3 Justification and the Church as Unmerited Gift of Grace and Challenge 16

2. **The Abiding Origin of the Church** 18

   2.1 Jesus Christ as the Only Foundation of the Church . . . 18

   2.2 The Election of Israel as the Abiding Presupposition of the Church 19

      2.2.1 God's Grace as the Continuum of Israel's History 20

      2.2.2 The Election of Israel for the Nations 20

   2.3 The Foundation of the Church in the Christ-event 21

      2.3.1 The Proclamation of the Reign of God in Word and Deed 22

      2.3.2 Cross and Resurrection 24

      2.3.3 The Church as the People of God from all Nations 27

   2.4 The Church as "Creature of the Gospel" 28

      2.4.1 The Proclamation of the Gospel as Foundation of the Church 28

      2.4.2 The Proclamation of the Gospel in the Holy Spirit 31

      2.4.3 The Proclamation of the Gospel by the Apostles . 32

3. **The Church of the Triune God** 35

   3.1 The Trinitarian Dimension of the Church 35

3.2 The Church as God's Pilgrim People, Body of Christ
and Temple of the Holy Spirit 36

   3.2.1 The Church as God's Pilgrim People 36
   3.2.2 The Church as Body of Christ 38
   3.2.3 The Church as Temple of the Holy Spirit. 40

3.3 The Church as *Koinonia/Communio* Founded in the
Trinity 41

   3.3.1 The Unity of the Church Sustained and Formed
       by the Triune God 41
   3.3.2 *Koinonia/Communio* through Preaching, Baptism
       and the Lord's Supper 43
   3.3.3 *Koinonia/Communio* as Anticipatory Reality. . . 45

3.4 Ecclesial Communion — Communion of Churches . . . 46

   3.4.1 Common Witness 46
   3.4.2 The Lutheran Understanding of Local Church . . 50
   3.4.3 The Roman Catholic Understanding of Local
       Church 52
   3.4.4 Tasks of Further Dialogue 59

4. The Church as Recipient and Mediator of Salvation . . . 60

4.1 The Church as *Congregatio Fidelium* 60

   4.1.1 The Lutheran View 61
   4.1.2 The Catholic View 63
   4.1.3 Common Witness 66

4.2 The Church as "Sacrament" of Salvation 66

   4.2.1 The Church under the Gospel and the Twofold
       Salvific Mediation of the Gospel 66
   4.2.2 The Catholic View 67
   4.2.3 The Lutheran View 71
   4.2.4 The Unity and Distinctness of Christ and the
       Church 73

4.3 The Church Visible and Hidden 75

4.4 Holy Church/Sinful Church 79

4.5 The Significance of the Doctrine of Justification for the
    Understanding of the Church 86

    4.5.1 The Problem and the Original Consensus 86
    4.5.2 Common Basic Convictions. 87
    4.5.3 The Areas of Controversy. 89
        4.5.3.1 Institutional Continuity of the Church . . 89
        4.5.3.2 Ordained Ministry as Institution in the
              Church 92
        4.5.3.3 Binding Church Doctrine and the Teach-
              ing Function of the Ministry 100
        4.5.3.4 Church Jurisdiction and the Jurisdic-
              tional Function of the Ministry 108

5. **The Mission and Consummation of the Church** 116

    5.1 The Church's Mission. 116

        5.1.1 Common Challenges to our Churches in a Con-
            stantly Changing World. 117
        5.1.2 Reflection on the Church's Mission in Light of
            the Message of Justification 119
        5.1.3 Mission as Sharing in God's Activity in the
            World 121
        5.1.3.1 Common Understanding 121
        5.1.3.2 Two Traditions 124
            5.1.3.2.1 The Lutheran Teaching on the
                  Two Kingdoms 124
            5.1.3.2.2 The Roman Catholic Teach-
                  ing on the "Proper Autonomy
                  of Earthly Affairs". 129
        5.1.4 The Fundamental Components of the Church's
            Missionary Task 131
        5.1.4.1 Commission to Evangelize 131
        5.1.4.2 Centrality of Worship 132
        5.1.4.3 Responsibility of the Church and the
              Service of Humanity 134

    5.2 The Eschatological Consummation of the Church. . . . 135

        5.2.1 *Sanctorum Communio* 136

5.2.1.1 Common Faith 136
5.2.1.2 Community of Perfected Saints 136
5.2.1.3 Communion of the Church on Earth with
         the Perfected Saints 137
5.2.2 The Church and the Kingdom of God 139
5.2.2.1 New Testament View 139
5.2.2.2 Lutheran View 140
5.2.2.3 Catholic View 141
5.2.2.4 Perspective in Ecumenical Dialogue . . 143
5.2.2.5 Common Witness 144

Members of the Lutheran-Roman Catholic Joint Commission . . 146

Foreword

Visible unity has always been and continues to be the ultimate goal of the international dialogue between the Roman Catholic Church and the Lutheran Communion. In 1992 this dialogue, sponsored by the Lutheran World Federation and the Pontifical Council for Promoting Christian Unity, celebrated its 25th anniversary, having begun its work in Zürich in 1967, just after the close of the Second Vatican Council.

With this document the dialogue completes the third phase of its work, a phase which has addressed an issue at the heart of Lutheran-Roman Catholic relations: the role of the Church in salvation. This theme grew organically out of the reports of the first two phases.

The Malta Report, *The Gospel and the Church* (1972), marked the end of the initial phase of dialogue. It ascertained a "far-reaching consensus" in the doctrine of justification and demonstrated a convergence of views in the area of Scripture and Tradition. The Malta Report became the foundation for further dialogue, establishing its direction and demonstrating its feasibility. The breadth of its scope led naturally to a series of documents in the second phase dealing with more particular dogmatic issues seen as church-dividing since the 16th century Reformation.

Having before it not only the confessional documents of the Reformation era, but also the documents of Vatican II, and benefiting from the labors of theologians in biblical, liturgical, dogmatic and historical studies, the Lutheran-Roman Catholic Joint Commission was able, in its second phase, to transmit to the churches common documents on *The Eucharist* (1978) and *The Ministry in the Church* (1981). It also produced statements marking two Reformation anniversaries: "All Under One Christ" was a common statement on the Confessio Augustana in observance of the 450th anniversary of its presentation in 1530, and "Martin Luther — Witness to Jesus Christ" was issued in 1983, the 500th anniversary of the Reformer's birth. Both documents and the many other articles and addresses that these anniversaries also occasioned are important contributions toward the goal of Catholic-Lutheran unity.

Two further documents from the second phase of dialogue addressed themselves to how visible unity might be realized in concrete ways: *Ways to Community* (1980) and *Facing Unity — Models, Forms and Phases of Catholic-Lutheran Church Fellowship* (1984).

When in 1985 the question of how to proceed to a third phase was addressed, a joint memorandum began with this judgment:

> The dialogue has brought us to a point from which it is no longer possible to go back. Thus the question about the actualization of Catholic-Lutheran church fellowship should be the framework for the further dialogue...

A statement from the 7th Assembly of the Lutheran World Federation (1984) was then quoted with approval:

> In the third phase of the continuing theological dialogue, the themes must be so formulated that the implications for church fellowship of the consensus expressed or the convergence achieved are clearly sought.

After a reference to the doctrinal condemnations of the Reformation era, the joint memorandum concludes:

> It can be observed that ... Catholics and Lutherans keep coming back to the question about the understanding of the church, more precisely to the central question of the church and the nature of its instrumentality in the divine plan of salvation (church as sign and instrument; "sacramentality" of the church) ... This question immediately raises again, especially for the Lutheran side, the question of the doctrine of justification. It is less a matter of the understanding of justification as such ... rather it is a matter of the implications of the mutual relationship of justification and the church.

8

It was noted how this brings the discussion back to an issue present already in the first phase of dialogue. Almost two decades later, however, the new Joint Commission had to take account of how the issue of justification had surfaced again in its documents on eucharist and ministry and be aware of the growing intensity of a new debate as to whether a "fundamental difference" between Protestantism and Catholicism really exists.

The third phase of dialogue was instructed to deal with the question of the church in light of sacramentality and justification. It began its work in the spring of 1986, completing it in 1993. Plenary sessions were held annually. In most years there was a drafting meeting scheduled between plenary sessions.

Once the work had begun it was the responsibility of the Joint Commission to shape, clarify and determine its own course. Though the joint statement here presented clearly follows the original mandate in the joint memorandum of 1985, two developments should be noted which may assist the reader in understanding our work. First, because of the developments between 1972 (Malta Report) and 1986, the Joint Commission found itself compelled to test the claim of a "far-reaching consensus" on justification. In so doing they relied heavily on the comprehensive American dialogue statement, *Justification by Faith* (1985), and on the justification chapter of *The Condemnations of the Reformation Era — Do They Still Divide?* (1986).

Second, as work progressed on what has become *Church and Justification*, ecclesiological themes not originally part of the schema required attention. The scope of the project had to grow if the result was to be persuasive. Thus it has become the most extensive statement to be presented by the international dialogue to date.

In submitting its work the Joint Commission asks that this report be seen together with the documents from the second phase *The Eucharist* and *The Ministry in the Church* as well as *Ways to Community* and *Facing Unity*. It asks whether, taken together, these documents constitute the sufficient consensus which would enable our churches to embark upon concrete steps toward visible unity which have become more and more urgent.

Würzburg, 11 September 1993

Paul-Werner Scheele
Bishop of Würzburg
Germany

James R. Crumley, Jr.
Bishop (retired)
Lutheran Church in America
USA

Abbreviations

AAS	*Acta Apostolica Sedis*
AG	*Ad Gentes*, Decree on the Church's Missionary Activity, in *The Documents of Vatican II*, Walter Abbott, S.J., General Editor, America Press/Association Press, 1966.
Apol	Apology of the Augsburg Confession (1531).
BC	*The Book of Concord*. The Confessions of the Evangelical Lutheran Church (tr. and ed. T. Tappert; Philadelphia: Fortress, 1959).
BEM	*Baptism, Eucharist and Ministry*, Faith and Order Paper No. 111, Geneva, 1982.
CA	Confessio Augustana (Augsburg Confession).
CD	*Christus Dominus*, Decree on the Bishops' Pastoral Office in the Church, in *The Documents of Vatican II*.
DH	*Dignitatis Humanae*, Declaration on Religious Freedom in *The Documents of Vatican II*.
DV	*Dei Verbum*, Dogmatic Constitution on Divine Revelation, in *The Documents of Vatican II*.
FC Ep	Formula of Concord (1577), Epitome.
FC SD	Formula of Concord (1577), Solid Declaration.
GS	*Gaudium et Spes*, Pastoral Constitution on the Church in the Modern World, in *The Documents of Vatican II*.
LC	The Large Catechism of Martin Luther (1529).
LG	*Lumen Gentium*, Dogmatic Constitution on the Church, in *The Documents of Vatican II*.
LW	*Luther's Works*, American Edition
LW Phil.Ed.	*Luther's Works*, Philadelphia Edition
NA	*Nostra Aetate*, Declaration on the Relationship of the Church to Non-Christian Religions, in *The Documents of Vatican II*.
PO	*Presbyterorum Ordinis*, Decree on the Ministry and Life of Priests, in *The Documents of Vatican II*.
SA	The Smalcald Articles (1537).
SC	*Sacrosanctum Concilium*, Constitution on the Sacred Liturgy, in *The Documents of Vatican II*.

UR	*Unitatis Redintegratio*, Decree on Ecumenism, in *The Documents of Vatican II.*
WA	Martin Luther, *Werke,* Weimarer Ausgabe.
WADB	WA Die Deutsche Bibel.

Bible quotations are taken from the New Revised Standard Version, 1989.

1. Justification and the Church

(1) Catholics and Lutherans in common believe in the triune God who for Christ's sake justifies sinners by grace through faith and makes them members of the church in baptism. Thus faith and baptism link justification and the church; the justified sinner is incorporated into the community of the faithful, the church, and becomes a member of it. Justification and the church thus stand in a vital relationship and are fruits of the saving activity of God.

(2) According to Lutheran tradition the justification of sinners is the article of faith by which the church stands or falls. [1] Thus Luther says in the exposition of Psalm 130:4, which for him is the epitome of the doctrine of justification: "for if this article stands, the Church stands; if it falls, the Church falls." [2] This is the background against which the Catholic-Lutheran Dialogue has as its theme the relation between justification and the church. A consensus in the doctrine of justification — even if it is nuanced — must prove itself ecclesiologically. Everything that is believed and taught about the nature of the church, the means of salvation and the church's ministry must be founded in the salvation-event itself and must be marked by justification-faith as the way in which the salvation-event is received and appropriated. Correspondingly, everything that is believed and taught about the nature and effect of justification must be understood in the overall context of statements about the church, the means of salvation and the church's ministry. This is the necessary precondition by which all the life and activity of the church must constantly be checked, as was stressed in the USA dialogue, *Justification by Faith*. "Catholics as well as Lutherans can acknowledge the need to test the practices, structures and theologies of the church by the extent to which they help or hinder 'the proclamation of God's free and merciful promises in Christ Jesus which can be rightly received only through faith'." [3]

---

[1] *Articulus stantis et cadentis ecclesiae.*
[2] WADB 40,III,352,3: *"quia isto articulo stante stat Ecclesia, ruente ruit Ecclesia."*
[3] *Justification by Faith*, Lutherans and Catholics in Dialogue VII, Minneapolis, 1985, 153.

(3) At the beginning of this dialogue document on the church in the light of justification-faith it should be emphasized that justification and the church are truths of faith (1.1) because both are grounded in faith in Christ and the Trinity (1.2) and are an unmerited gift of grace which becomes at the same time a challenge in our world (1.3).

1.1 Justification and the Church as Truths of Faith

(4) Catholics and Lutherans together testify to the salvation that is bestowed only in Christ and by grace alone and is received in faith. They recite in common the creed, confessing "one holy catholic and apostolic church." Both the justification of sinners and the church are fundamental articles of faith. In faith in the triune God we confess that this God justifies us by grace without our meriting it and gathers us together in his church. His mercy is and remains the source of our life. "Solely by grace and by faith in Christ's saving work and not because of any merit in us ... we are accepted by God and receive the Holy Spirit who renews our hearts and equips us for and calls us to good works."[4] It is by God's incomprehensible "glorious grace" that we have access through Christ in one Spirit to the Father, "are citizens with the saints and also members of the household of God" and "are built together spiritually into a dwelling place for God" (Eph 2:18-22; cf. Eph 1:5f).

(5) Strictly and properly speaking, we do not believe in justification and in the church but in the Father who has mercy on us and who gathers us in the church as his people; and in Christ who justifies us and whose body the church is; and in the Holy Spirit who sanctifies us and dwells in the church. Our faith encompasses justification and the church as works of the triune God which can be properly accepted only in faith in him. We believe in justification and the church as a *mysterium*, a mystery of faith, because we believe solely in God, to whom alone we may completely consign our lives in freedom and

---

[4] *All Under One Christ*, 1980, Statement on the Augsburg Confession by the Roman Catholic/Lutheran Joint Commission, 14, in Harding Meyer and Lukas Vischer, eds., *Growth in Agreement,* New York/Geneva, 1982, 241-247.

love and in whose word alone, which promises salvation, we can establish our whole life with complete trust. Consequently we can say in common that justification and the church both guide us into the mystery of the triune God and are therefore *mysterium*, the mystery of faith, hope and love.

1.2 Justification and the Church Founded in the Mystery of Christ and of the Trinity

(6) According to the witness of the New Testament, our salvation, the justification of sinners and the existence of the church are indissolubly linked with the triune God and are founded in him alone. This is attested in various but consistent ways. "God ... proves his love for us in that while we still were sinners Christ died for us. ... Now that we have been justified by his blood, will we be saved through him from the wrath of God. For if while we were enemies, we were reconciled to God through the death of his Son, much more surely, having been reconciled, will we be saved by his life" (Rom 5:8-10). "For God so loved the world that he gave his only Son, so that everyone who believes in him may not perish but may have eternal life" (Jn 3:16). "In this is love, not that we loved God but that he loved us and sent his Son to be the atoning sacrifice for our sins" (1 Jn 4:10). In short, God "first loved us" (1 Jn 4:19). Our salvation in the triune God is founded in the sending of the Son and of the Holy Spirit (cf. Gal 4:4-6; Jn 14:16f,26; 16:7-15).

(7) Accordingly, the church has its foundation in the sacrifice of the Son and the sending of the Spirit. God "obtained" his church "with the blood of his own Son" (Acts 20:28). Christ has saved the church for it is his body (cf. Eph 5:23). Christ "loved the church and gave himself up for her, in order to make her holy by cleansing her with the washing of water by the word" (Eph 5:25f). By virtue of the sending of the Holy Spirit the young church appears publicly on the day of Pentecost (cf. Acts 2). Especially in Paul's letters, the relation of the church to the triune God becomes clear, when he describes it as the pilgrim people of God the Father, as the body of Christ, the Son, and as the temple of the Holy Spirit.

1.3 Justification and the Church as Unmerited Gift of Grace and Challenge

(8) When Paul describes God's church in Corinth as "those who are sanctified in Christ Jesus, called to be saints" he shows by this that the church and its members live entirely by the unmerited gift of Christ's grace, for which he expressly gives thanks (1 Cor 1:2-4). In the letter to the Ephesians the unmerited gift of grace which constitutes both Christian existence and the church becomes an occasion for the praise of God's majesty and grace (cf. Eph 1:3-14). "For by grace you have been saved through faith, and this is not your own doing; it is the gift of God — not the result of works, so that no one may boast" (Eph 2:8f). The mystery of Christ and of the Trinity is the foundation for this unmerited gracious gift of justification and the church: "But when the goodness and loving kindness of God our Savior appeared, he saved us, not because of any works of righteousness that we had done, but according to his mercy, through the water of rebirth and renewal by the Holy Spirit. This Spirit he poured out on us richly through Jesus Christ our Savior, so that, having been justified by his grace, we might become heirs according to the hope of eternal life" (Titus 3:4-7). It corresponds to the graciousness of this gift that human beings contribute nothing but can only receive it in faith: "For by grace you have been saved through faith" (Eph 2:8; cf. Rom 3:28).

(9) Lutherans and Catholics together acknowledge the biblical witness on justification and the church as an unmerited gift of grace; they see in this witness a tremendous challenge in our world. God "desires everyone to be saved and to come to the knowledge of the truth" (1 Tim 2:4). The message of justification is an expression of God's universal saving will. It promises salvation and the right to life without regard to merit and worthiness. God accepts the sinful creature in pure mercy and thus cancels out the law of works and achievement as the basis for life. God thus opens up a way of life which most profoundly contradicts that which prevails in the world: the life of love. This love arises out of faith and passes on the boundless mercy which it has received. It suffers from the distress and injustice that others experience and meets it with self-sacrifice and

renunciation. And it urges the members of the church to promote justice, peace and the integrity of creation together with all people of good will amid the glaring contrast between poor and rich, and in the conflicts between ideologies and interests, races, nations and sexes. Thus the church is both a contradiction and a challenge in our world — as the place where merciful justification is proclaimed, as the locus for community and love, as co-shaper of a more just and humane world.

2. The Abiding Origin of the Church

2.1 Jesus Christ as the Only Foundation of the Church

(10) "No one can lay any foundation other than the one that has been laid; that foundation is Jesus Christ" (1 Cor 3:11). In all its trenchancy this statement is to be evaluated and heeded as the fundamental principle of ecclesiology. "The one and only foundation of the church is the saving work of God in Jesus Christ which has taken place once for all."[5] Everything that is to be said on the origin, nature and purpose of the church must be understood as an explanation of this principle. As an essential mark of the church, its unity — which since the very beginning of church history has existed only as a unity under threat, challenged by fragmentation (cf. 1 Cor 1:10ff) — is to be understood solely in the light of this principle.

(11) "Jesus the Christ" or "Jesus is Lord" is the original form of the Christian confession of faith. The author of this confession, through which the church as community becomes heard in this world, is the Holy Spirit, in whose power Christ is known as the Lord (1 Cor 12:3), and God the Father, who by his revelation gives us faith in the Messiah and Son (cf. Mt 16:17). The church owes its origin "not to a single, isolated act by which it was established" but is "founded in the totality of the Christ-event ... starting from the election of the people of God of the Old Testament, in the work of Jesus, in his proclamation of the kingdom and in the gathering of the disciples through his call to conversion and discipleship, ... in the institution of the Lord's Supper, in the cross and resurrection of Christ, in the outpouring of the Holy Spirit and in the fact that this whole path is directed towards eschatological consummation in the *parousia* of the Lord."[6] In this comprehensive sense, the term "founding or institution of the church

---

[5] *Kirchengemeinschaft in Wort und Sakrament*. Bilaterale Arbeitsgruppe der Deutschen Bischofskonferenz und der Kirchenleitung der Vereinigten Evangelisch-Lutherischen Kirche Deutschlands, Paderborn/Hannover, 1984, 1 (hereafter: Kirchengemeinschaft).

[6] *Ibid*. 2; cf. LG 3f.

by Jesus Christ" is a meaningful explication of the ecclesiological principle in 1 Cor 3:11, which cannot be abandoned.

(12) Jesus' whole work is determined and permeated by the mystery of the Trinity. It was always in obedience to the Father who sent him (cf. Jn 5:19); it was also filled with the authority and power of the Holy Spirit through whom Jesus had his existence (cf. Lk 1:35), who showed him to be the Son of God from his baptism onwards (cf. Lk 3:22) and who revealed him with power by resurrection from the dead (cf. Rom 1:4). Thus the trinitarian confession was already included in the original form of the confession of Christ, as a doxology of the work of salvation which has taken place once for all.

2.2 The Election of Israel as the Abiding Presupposition of the Church

(13) The church of the New Testament was always aware that the history of the people of God did not begin with itself. The God who raised Jesus from the dead is the same God who called Abraham to be the father of all who believe, who elected Israel from among all the nations to be his treasured possession and who entered into an enduring covenant with it (cf. Rom 9:6). In salvation-history the church thus presupposes the history of Israel (cf. Acts 13:16ff; Heb 1:1f). "The Church ever keeps in mind the words of the Apostle about his kinsmen, 'who have the adoption as sons, and the glory and the covenant and the legislation and the worship and the promises; who have the fathers, and from whom is Christ according to the flesh' (Rom 9:4-5), the son of the virgin Mary."[7] The church must always remain conscious of the fact that "she received the revelation of the Old Testament through the people with whom God in his inexpressible mercy deigned to establish the Ancient Covenant. Nor can she forget that she draws sustenance from the root of that good olive tree onto which have been grafted the wild olive branches of the Gentiles (cf. Rom 11:17-24)."[8]

[7] NA 4.
[8] *Ibid.*

2.2.1 God's Grace as the Continuum of Israel's History

(14) God communicated to Israel the mystery of his name and assured them "I am the Lord your God" (Ex 20:2). "You only have I known of all the families of the earth" (Am 3:2; cf. Deut 7:6). For that purpose God already called Abraham from his father's house and his homeland (cf. Gen 12:1) into a path of obedient faith in him who called him (cf. Gen 15:6; 17:1). Israel's faithfulness was not to be divided: "You must remain completely loyal to the Lord your God" (Deut 18:13). Israel shall therefore not have any other gods but serve only the one and only true God (cf. Ex 20:3-5). "Hear, O Israel: The Lord is our God, the Lord alone. You shall love the Lord your God with all your heart, and with all your soul, and with all your might" (Deut 6:4f). This was and is Israel's fundamental confession.

(15) God's choice of Israel from among all the nations as his own people is not based on its merits or outstanding achievements. "It was not because you were more numerous than any other people that the Lord set his heart on you and chose you — for you were the fewest of all peoples. It was because the Lord loved you ... that the Lord has brought you out with a mighty hand" (Deut 7:7f). This love remains steadfast. Though Israel often broke its covenant faith with God, God remained open to its conversion. Where God might have rightly terminated the covenant or said to Israel, as to an adulterer, "You are not my people," he called them to himself with the loving words, "Children of the living God" (Hos 1:10; cf. Rom 9:25f). Thus the miracle of the forgiveness of sins belongs to the gifts of God's love for his people (cf. Is 44:2). From the start God's covenant faithfulness includes the forgiveness of sins. Many psalms testify to this, just as the prophets not only proclaim judgment but repeatedly testify also to grace and return. God's grace is the origin and foundation of the Old and the New Covenants and the basis for the expectation of eternal glory.

2.2.2 The Election of Israel for the Nations

(16) Although God's saving concern was repeatedly rejected and the covenant broken, God himself preserved the continuity of his

gracious care by ever-renewed saving initiatives. And just as the covenant with Noah established a new start in humanity's history with God, so too the election of Israel from the beginning aimed at the inclusion of all nations in God's salvation history.

(17) The blessing God promised Abraham is not limited to making his descendants a great nation but has its climax in the promise, "... in you all the families of the earth shall be blessed" (Gen 12:3; cf. Gal 3:8). The prophets see as the final act of salvation-history the nations of the earth moving to Jerusalem like a star-shaped pilgrimage from every direction, to receive a common salvation in God's universal kingdom of peace (cf. Is 2:1-5; Mic 4:1-4). Zion as the center of Israel is to become the center of the messianic kingdom of peace for the whole world of nations, and a descendant of David, the great king of Israel, is to be the king of peace ruling over all the nations (cf. Is 9:5f). As the chosen Servant of God, he himself will bring the justice of God to the peoples of the whole earth (cf. Is 42:1-12; 49:6).

2.3 The Foundation of the Church in the Christ-event

(18) "But when the fullness of time had come, God sent his Son, born of a woman, born under the law, in order to redeem those who were under the law, so that we might receive adoption as children. And because you are children, God has sent the Spirit of his Son into our hearts, crying, 'Abba! Father!'" (Gal 4:4-6). Jesus' mother was a Jewish woman. As the Messiah of Israel Jesus is descended from the family of David (cf. Lk 1:32f; Rom 1:3f). The God whose rule Jesus proclaimed is the God of Abraham, Isaac and Jacob. It was to the people of Israel that Jesus directed this proclamation (cf. Mt 15:24; 10:6). Jesus proclaimed God's love in an unheard-of radical way: "I have come to call not the righteous but sinners" (Mk 2:17). In line with this he taught love for this God whose kingly rule is consummated in mercy and the love of one's neighbor, including enemies (cf. Mt 5:44). On these two fundamental commandments "hang" all the law and the prophets (Mt 22:40; cf. Deut 6:5; Lev 19:18).

(19) That Jesus as Son of God is the Messiah and that in him the eschatological rule of God has dawned is the unique saving event which effects a definitive salvation for all the nations, going beyond all the saving gifts in the history of his people. All the promises of the prophets are fulfilled in him: he is the light that illumines all darkness; the life that overcomes all the power of death, the righteousness that cancels out all sin. According to the witness of the New Testament the "new covenant" (Jer 31:31-34) has been inaugurated in his "blood" (1 Cor 11:25; Lk 22:20), and his blood is the "blood of the covenant" (Ex 24:8) which was poured out for all "for the forgiveness of sins" (Mt 26:28; cf. Mk 14:24). In Jesus is perfected God's faithfulness to the covenant. From the beginning God has held fast to his will to save, against all human unfaithfulness: "... God has imprisoned all in disobedience so that he may be merciful to all" (Rom 11:32).

2.3.1 The Proclamation of the Reign of God in Word and Deed

(20) What Jesus proclaimed was the dawn of the exclusive reign of God (cf. Psalm 97), which was looked for by Israel, sung in the "new song" (Psalm 96), but effected in an entirely unexpected way. In many parables Jesus speaks pointedly of its nearness in figures of speech. It is like a tiny seed out of which a great tree will grow (cf. Mt 13:31f). It is like a "treasure hidden in a field" or an incomparably beautiful pearl, which should be acquired here and now and for which one will spend no less than everything one has (Mt 13:44-46). It comes up and grows "of itself;" human effort can neither aid it in any way (Mk 4:26-29) nor prevent what it does (cf. Mt 13:24-26). It is God's action alone. But all those who accept it from Jesus' words and deeds must allow themselves to be wholly taken into service by it and must subordinate everything else to it (cf. Lk 9:57-62).

(21) The reign of God is present in Jesus' words and deeds. By virtue of "the Spirit of God" he expels demons (Mt 12:28) and frees human beings from their power (cf. Mk 5:1ff). It is the saving power of God's eschatological reign that Jesus promises to sinners (cf. Mk 2:10f). "I have come to call not the righteous but sinners" (Mk 2:17; cf. Lk 18:9ff). In common meals in which eschatological joy of salvation prevails, he celebrates the miracle of the presence of the

kingdom of God with "tax collectors and sinners" (Mk 2:15f). These meals are also harbingers of the eucharistic community of the church after Easter.

(22) What Jesus proclaims as the power of God's reign is his justifying love which creates salvation: his unlimited mercy, with which he receives the lost into his Father's house and bestows rich gifts on them (cf. Lk 15:11ff), forgives sinners their guilt (cf. Mt 18:23ff), promises salvation to the poor, the hungry and the suffering (cf. Lk 6:20-23) and gives the last the same share in his salvation as the first (cf. Mt 20:1ff). Correspondingly, the unlimited love of one's neighbor is the real meaning of the righteousness that God calls for from his elect (cf. Lk 10:25-37). Thus in the Sermon on the Mount Jesus shows us the actual intention of God's law in its individual commandments. Just as the reign of God redeems the lost, so too it lays on those who are saved the duty of solidarity with the lost as "peacemakers" (Mt 5:9), and prepares them to accept persecutions, slanders and sufferings "for righteousness' sake" (Mt 5:10-12).

(23) Jesus called specific persons to follow him as his disciples. Thus they became personal witnesses to the nearness of the reign of God. That reign is to be accepted at once, without delay and apprehensiveness (cf. Lk 14:15ff; 17:28ff). The disciples are to leave everything (cf. Mk 1:16ff; 10:29f) in order to be fully with Jesus (cf. Mk 3:14) and follow him wherever he goes. Self-denial is as much a mark of citizenship in the kingdom of God (cf. Mt 18:3f) as following Jesus (cf. Mk 8:34).

(24) Jesus called twelve disciples as his particular followers. He sent them out and empowered them as his messengers (apostles) to proclaim his message of the kingdom of God to the whole people of Israel and, as a sign of its nearness, to heal the sick and free the possessed from the power of the demons just as he had done (cf. Mk 3:14f; 6:7; Mt 10:7f). That the apostles numbered twelve corresponds to the full complement of the tribes of Israel. Thus their ministry has a meaning in terms of salvation-history: in the proclamation of Jesus the kingdom of God has definitively dawned, that kingdom which is the consummation of God's history with his chosen people, however

much its ultimate manifestation on the last day is still pending. But at the same time the ministry of the twelve apostles also has a fundamental ecclesial significance. The apostles are to preach the gospel after Easter so that their witness is foundational and normative for the whole church. According to Luke 10:1 Jesus also sent out 70 (or 72) other disciples with the same mission. Their number matches that of "the elders of Israel" (Ex 24:1; Num 11:16f) and relates likewise to the people of Israel as a whole and to the full complement of the nations (cf. Gen 10).

(25) The kingdom of God is the eschatological saving reality that affects the whole world. In earthly terms it is unattainable. Nevertheless because it is there in Jesus, it is present among his disciples (cf. Lk 17:20f). The same is also true of the church: it is not identical with the kingdom of God, which even after Easter remains hidden in the eschatological future. The kingdom is entirely God's affair, not that of any human being nor is it at the disposal of anyone in the church. And yet its eschatological saving reality can already be experienced in the church in the "righteousness and peace and joy" which, imparted by word and sacrament, take effect in the common life of Christians "in the Holy Spirit" (Rom 14:17). In this sense it can be said that the church is the kingdom of God already present but "hidden"[9] "in mystery"[10].

2.3.2 Cross and Resurrection

(26) Jesus, who taught his disciples to pray for protection from eschatological sufferings (cf. Mt 6:13; Lk 11:4), who was aware of the provocation of his message (cf. Mt 10:34-36) and who proclaimed the reign of God in weakness (cf. Mt 11:12; Mk 4:30-32 par), was himself willing to accept the consequences arising from his preaching. He himself lived out the willingness to serve to the end and the readiness for martyrdom which he demanded from his disciples (cf. Lk 22:27; Mk 9:35 par; Mk 8:34f). When he journeyed up to

---

[9] Apol 7,17f; BC 171.
[10] LG 3.

Jerusalem, he knew what had befallen John the Baptist and was aware of the fate of the prophets (cf. Mk 6:14-29; 9:13; Mt 23:34-39). In regard to the aim of his mission he was able to say: "For the Son of Man came not to be served but to serve, and to give his life a ransom for many" (Mk 10:45; cf. 1 Tim 2:5)[11]. In unwavering confidence that the reign of God was coming (cf. Mk 14:25), he voluntarily took upon himself (cf. Mt 26:39,42) his death on the cross as a necessity (cf. Mk 8:31; 9:31; 10:32f) laid upon him in accordance with God's saving will and suffered the distress of being forsaken by God (cf. Mk 15:34; Mt 27:46). In this he fulfilled the prophecy of the Servant of God who "bore the sin of many" (Is 53:12): "But he was wounded for our transgressions, crushed for our iniquities; upon him was the punishment that made us whole, and by his bruises we are healed" (Is 53:5; cf. 1 Pet 2:24; Rom 4:25).

(27) In the night before his death, at supper together with the Twelve, Jesus "took a loaf of bread and after blessing it he broke it, gave it to them, and said, 'Take, this is my body.' Then he took a cup, and after giving thanks he gave it to them, and all of them drank from it. He said to them, 'This is my blood of the covenant, which is poured out for many'" (Mk 14:22-24). Thus with effective signs Jesus gave his disciples an anticipatory share in the saving event of his atoning death as a once-for-all sacrifice, through which all who believe in him have been redeemed from sin (cf. Mt 26:28) and freed for life in the Spirit. According to the formulations in Mark and Matthew, that which happened for Israel in the action of the covenant made at Sinai (Ex 24:8) now happens "for many." According to the formulations in Luke and Paul (cf. 1 Cor 11:25) the prophetic promise of the New Covenant (cf. Jer 31:31-34) is realized. The meaning is the same: the eschatological miracle of a universal "eternal redemption" (Heb 9:12) takes place in Jesus' sacrificial death on the cross. With the command, "Do this in remembrance of me" (1 Cor 11:24f; Lk 22:19), Jesus promises his church that in every celebration of the Lord's Supper he himself will be present as the one who was sacrificed for us, in the same way as in this meal with the apostles on

---

[11] Kirchengemeinschaft, 2; LG 5.

the Passover Eve before his death: "For as often as you eat this bread and drink the cup, you proclaim the Lord's death until he comes" (1 Cor 11:26).

(28) For the disciples the story of Jesus' Passion becomes the story of their denial. They fell asleep while Jesus, in his prayer that night, struggled with the will of his heavenly Father (cf. Mk 14:37-41). Upon his arrest they all fled (cf. Mk 14:50). Even Simon, the "Rock", goes back on his word: having just been willing to share death and prison with his Master (cf. Lk 22:23), he denies him three times (cf. Mk 14:66ff). Only Jesus' prayer for him keeps him from falling into Satan's control and brings him back to faith, thereafter to strengthen his brothers (cf. Lk 22:31ff; Jn 21:15ff). Abandoned by everyone in Gethsemane, Jesus accepted his own death, surrendering in complete faith to his Father, so that "he became the source of eternal salvation for all who obey him" as "a high priest according to the order of Melchizedek" (Heb 5:7-10). Thus in every act of worship Christ's congregation goes to that cross "outside the gate" that there they may bear his shame (Heb 13:10-12) and have that communion with the crucified which takes us beyond earthly time into the "city that is to come" (Heb 13:14).

(29) Jesus' mother stands below the cross with two other women and the "disciple whom he loved" (Jn 19:25-27). Jesus commends them to each other: the disciple to Mary as her son in his stead and Mary to the disciple as his mother. Thus in the form of these two a small community stands under Jesus' cross as archetype of the church whose permanent place is the cross of its Lord whence it has its life. After Jesus' death a soldier pierced his side "and at once blood and water came out" (Jn 19:34) — a sign that the saving effect of his death would benefit his church through the sacraments of baptism and the Lord's Supper (cf. 1 Jn 5:5-8).

(30) In the early hours of Easter morning three women disciples find Jesus' grave empty, and an angel announces his resurrection (cf. Mk 16:1ff). The risen Christ himself "appeared to Cephas, then to the twelve" (1 Cor 15:5) and frequently to still others, men and women. The resurrection of the crucified is God's central eschatological

miracle, the break-through of the eschaton: Jesus is "the first fruits of those who have died," the first to experience resurrection (1 Cor 15:20; cf. Col 1:18): he is God's act of new creation, through which he has procured victory for the love with which his Son gave himself to us (cf. 1 Cor 15:57; Rom 8:31-39; Col 2:13f). By this act of God's power, the death of Christ has acquired saving power: as the justification of sinners (cf. Rom 4:25) and as reconciliation with God (cf. 2 Cor 5:18-21) as well as a new creation — life in the power of the Spirit (cf. 2 Cor 5:17; Rom 8:9-11; Eph 2:5f; 1 Pet 1:2). In his exaltation above "every name" (Phil 2:9-11) the risen Lord has become "head of the body, the church" (Col 1:18) and has become lord over the entire universe, a lordship which will last till he hands over the universe — reconciled and at peace — to his Father, and God becomes "all in all" (1 Cor 15:25-28).

(31) Before his exaltation to the Father, for his disciples Jesus opened up the understanding of Scripture as witness to Christ, its center being his suffering on the cross and his resurrection (cf. Lk 24:45f). He gave the apostles the commission and authority to preach the gospel of repentance for "the forgiveness of sins ... to all nations" (Lk 24:47) : "Go therefore and make disciples of all nations, baptizing them in the name of the Father and of the Son and of the Holy Spirit, and teaching them to obey everything that I have commanded you. And remember, I am with you always, to the end of the age" (Mt 28:19f). As a legacy he gave his church the Holy Spirit which was to "guide" them "into all the truth" (Jn 16:13), empower them to forgive sins (cf. Jn 20:23) and enable them to preach and bear witness among all the nations (cf. Acts 1:8). In the power of the Spirit of God the church was to abide in the love of Christ as he abides in his Father's love (cf. Jn 14:16f; 15:10) — "that they may all be one" so that the world may know that Jesus Christ is the Son sent by the Father who loves his own as the Father loves him (Jn 17:21-23).

2.3.3 The Church as the People of God from all Nations

(32) The wonderful plan of God's salvation-history is that in Jesus' mission that purpose is also fulfilled which from the beginning

God had linked to the election of Israel: the inclusion of all nations in the promised salvation and the foundation of the church as God's eschatological community of salvation. Just as at the beginning God recognized Abraham's righteousness without merit or worthiness but on the basis of faith alone (cf. Gen 15:6; Rom 4:3-8), so too he has made the same justification "by faith apart from works prescribed by the law" (Rom 3:28) the entrance into his church for everyone (cf. Rom 4:16f; Gal 3:6-9). Jesus Christ is the one Lord of the one church from among all the nations (cf. Acts 10:34-36), the one foundation and cornerstone of what God has built (cf. Eph 2:20f). Abraham's faith in the God who justifies sinners is fulfilled in the faith of Christians in Jesus Christ (cf. Rom 4:3).

(33) In the outpouring of the Spirit on the day of Pentecost, God confirms that the assembly of those who believe in Jesus as the Christ is God's messianic people of the last days (cf. Acts 2; 1 Cor 12-14; Jn 14:15-31; 16:4-15; 20:19-23). Therefore the apostle's proclamation of the gospel "concerning his Son" (Rom 1:3) serves to "bring about the obedience of faith among all ..." (Rom 1:5). Paul is not ashamed of the gospel which "is the power of God for salvation to everyone who has faith, to the Jew first and also to the Greek. For in it the righteousness of God is revealed through faith for faith; as it is written, 'The one who is righteous will live by faith'" (Rom 1:16f). In this way Paul unfolds the gospel concerning the Son, identifying it with the gospel of the righteousness of God.

2.4   The Church as "Creature of the Gospel"

2.4.1   The Proclamation of the Gospel as Foundation of the Church

(34) As on earth the Lord called and gathered people by the proclamation of the "good news of the kingdom" (Mt 4:23; 9:35; 24:14; Mk 1:14) so too after Pentecost the calling and the fresh gathering of God's people is continued by the proclamation of the "good news of Christ" (Rom 15:19; cf. 1:16; 1:1-9). For this purpose

the risen Lord chooses his witnesses and sends them into the world (cf. Mt 28:19; Mk 16:15; Acts 1:8; Jn 20:21). When they proclaim the gospel of "Jesus as the Messiah" (Acts 5:42) and people hear that gospel and accept it in faith as a promise of salvation, congregations are constituted from Jerusalem as far as Rome. The commission laid upon the apostles is "to proclaim the gospel" (Rom 1:15; 1 Cor 1:17; 9:16). This gospel, as "God's word" (1 Thess 2:13) or the "word of the Lord" calls people to be "imitators of ... the Lord" (1 Thess 1:5-8) and brings the church into being (cf. 1 Cor 15:1f).

(35) At the side of the audible word of gospel proclamation stand baptism and the Lord's Supper as visible means of God's saving acts and of the gathering of his people (cf. 1 Cor 10:1-13). Just as a rescued Israel emerges out of the Red Sea, so the Christian community emerges out of baptism; as the manna was for Israel in the desert, so now the Lord's Supper is the pilgrim food for God's new people. Through baptism all are bound together with Christ (cf. Rom 6:3ff) and form the one "body of Christ" (1 Cor 12:27). The Lord's Supper is par excellence the visible and effectual expression of the congregation as a "sharing in the body of Christ" (1 Cor 10:16f).

(36) The sixteenth century Reformation highlighted with utmost emphasis the fact that the church lives on the basis of the proclamation of the gospel. It reproached the church of that time for not corresponding to that fundamental dependence on the gospel in its life and doctrine, and for having to a great extent withdrawn itself from subordination to the gospel. Consequently the main ecclesiological concern of the Reformation was perpetual dependence on the gospel and subordination to it. This was concentrated in the formula that the church is *creatura Evangelii*. [12] Already in 1517 the 62nd of Luther's 95 theses spoke of "the most holy gospel" [13] as "the true treasure of the church" [14] and one of the key principles of Lutheran ecclesiology takes this up: "The entire life and nature of the church is in the word of

---

[12] WA 2,430.
[13] WA 1,236: *sacrosanctum evangelium*; LW 31,31.
[14] *Ibid.*: *Verus thesaurus ecclesie*; ibid.

God."[15] Article 7 of the Augsburg Confession corresponds to this, describing the church as "the assembly of all believers among whom the Gospel is preached in its purity and the holy sacraments are administered according to the Gospel."[16]

(37) The conviction that the church lives out of the gospel also determines the Roman Catholic understanding of the church. In Vatican II's Dogmatic Constitution on the Church we read, "... the gospel ... is for all time the source of all life for the Church;"[17] and the Decree on the Church's Missionary Activity says that the "chief means of this implantation [i.e., of the church] is the preaching of the gospel of Jesus Christ."[18] The Apostolic Exhortation of Pope Paul VI, *Evangelization in the Modern World* states, "The Church is born of the evangelizing activity of Jesus and the Twelve. ... Having been born consequently out of being sent, the Church in her turn is sent by Jesus. ... Having been sent and evangelized, the Church herself sends out evangelizers. [They are] to preach not their own selves or their personal ideas, but a Gospel of which neither she nor they are the absolute masters and owners, to dispose of it as they wish, but a Gospel of which they are the ministers, in order to pass it on with complete fidelity."[19]

(38) In the Malta Report Catholics and Lutherans together said that the church "as *creatura et ministra verbi* ... stands under the gospel and has the gospel as its superordinate criterion."[20] There was agreement that "the authority of the church can only be service of the word and ... it is not master of the word of the Lord."[21] This primacy of the gospel over the church was also attested jointly in regard to church order and the ministry.[22]

---

[15] WA 7,721.
[16] CA 7, BC 32.
[17] LG 20.
[18] AG 6.
[19] *Evangelii Nuntiandi*, 1975, 15.
[20] Report of the Joint Lutheran-Roman Catholic Study Commission on "The Gospel and the Church," 1972, 48 (hereafter: Malta Report), in *Growth in Agreement*, 168-189.
[21] *Ibid.* 21.
[22] *Ibid.* 33, 47, 48, 50; cf. 56.

(39) For the Reformation it was self-evident that the proclamation of the gospel as the imparting of grace and salvation does not take place only in the preached word. Even when the Reformers were particularly stressing the importance of proclaiming the word, they held fast to the idea that the gospel is also communicated through the sacraments and that the preached word and administered sacraments belong together. The Smalcald Articles state that the "Gospel" is not proclaimed "in ... one way" but "through the spoken word," "through Baptism," "through the holy Sacrament of the Altar" and "through the power of the keys."[23] The definition of the church as *creatura Evangelii* therefore means that the church lives on the basis of the gospel that is communicated in word and sacrament and accepted through faith.

(40) Imparting the gospel in word and sacrament implies the ministry of proclaiming the word and administering the sacraments. This corresponds to the biblical witness according to which the message of reconciliation implies the "ministry of reconciliation" (2 Cor 5:18ff). Proclaiming the word and administering the sacraments are therefore not merely momentary acts but fundamental realities which permanently define the church. While all believers are to communicate the gospel in their own spheres of life, the proclamation of the word and the administration of the sacraments as public acts are perpetually assigned to the ministry instituted by God. A basic agreement exists here between Catholic and Lutheran teaching, notwithstanding the existing differences in how this ministry is understood and organized. This has been repeatedly ascertained by the Catholic-Lutheran Dialogue: "By church we mean the communion of those whom God gathers together through Christ in the Holy Spirit, by the proclamation of the gospel and the administration of the sacraments, and the ministry instituted by him for this purpose."[24]

2.4.2   The Proclamation of the Gospel in the Holy Spirit

(41) We share the belief that the Holy Spirit creates the church as the communion of believers through faith in the gospel and works

[23] SA III,4; BC 310.
[24] *All Under One Christ*, 16.

through this communion. The proclamation of the gospel takes place in the power of the Holy Spirit (cf. Acts 1:8). It comes "in power and in the Holy Spirit and with full conviction" and makes those who accept the word themselves messengers of the gospel (1 Thess 1:5-8). The Holy Spirit who is promised and given to those who bear witness to the gospel (cf. Jn 20:22) empowers them for their witness (cf. 2 Cor 4:13), keeps them with Christ (cf. Jn 14:26; 15:26f) and gives them the certainty of acting not in their own strength but "for Christ" (2 Cor 5:20) and with his authority (cf. Jn 20:23).

(42) The Holy Spirit who calls and empowers witnesses for gospel testimony also awakens and sustains the faith which responds to the proclaimed gospel, faith which accepts it as the promise of salvation (cf. 1 Thess 1:5f; 1 Tim 1:14). It is the Spirit who enables those who hear the message to confess Christ as Lord (cf. 1 Cor 12:3; Rom 10:9f). In this "Spirit of adoption," they have access to God through Christ and call him "Father" (Rom 8:14-16; Eph 2:18).

(43) In awakening faith through the proclaimed gospel the Holy Spirit brings the church into being (cf. Acts 2), as congregations who are known and commended for their faith (cf. Rom 1:8; 1 Thess 1:8). Through the Spirit all are "baptized into one body" (1 Cor 12:13). In the variety of gifts the Spirit binds the individual believers together as living members (cf. 1 Cor 12:4ff). The unity of the Spirit is also the principle of the unity of this body that is the church (cf. 1 Cor 12:13; Eph 4:3f), which as a whole is a "dwelling place for God" in the Spirit (Eph 2:22).

2.4.3   The Proclamation of the Gospel by the Apostles

(44) That Jesus Christ is the church's "foundation" (1 Cor 3:11) and that the church lives on the basis of the gospel of Christ is concretized in the fact that the apostles called by Christ are also the church's "foundation" (Eph 2:20). This they are not of themselves but by the power of the gospel which they have received and to which they are primary witnesses — the gospel transmitted in word and sacrament that creates, sustains and governs the church. This has

permanent eschatological validity. The twelve apostles of Jesus will "sit on twelve thrones, judging the twelve tribes of Israel" (Mt 19:28 par), and the "twelve foundations" bear "the twelve names of the twelve apostles of the Lamb" (Rev 21:14).

(45) In the ancient church appealing to the apostles and their testimony was the decisive defense against false doctrine. "We have learned from none others the plan of our salvation, than from those [i.e., the apostles] through whom the Gospel has come down to us."[25] As the apostles received the revelation from Christ so too the church receives it through the apostles[26] and the "rule of faith" acquires its binding nature through its faithful reflection of this apostolic tradition.[27] Augustine sums up: "What the whole church believes is wholly rightly believed, even if it has not been directly decided by councils, but has been transmitted only on apostolic authority as belonging to the unquestioned substance of the faith."[28] The title of the creed as the "Apostles Creed"[29] expresses this conviction of the abiding, binding nature of the apostolic witness.

(46) This apostolic testimony — according to the common conviction of our churches — has its normative expression in the New Testament canon. All subsequent church proclamation, doctrine and tradition is interpretation. As apostolic writings the scriptures of the New Testament, together with those of the Old Testament are "the only rule and norm according to which all doctrines and teachers alike must be appraised and judged" say the Lutheran Confessions.[30] The Dogmatic Constitution on Divine Revelation of Vatican II states that the apostles had the commission to "preach to all men the gospel" as "the source of all saving truth and moral teaching."[31] Hence "apos-

---

[25] Irenaeus, "Against Heresies," III.1.1 in *Ante-Nicene Fathers*, Grand Rapids, Michigan, 1967, 1,414.

[26] Cf. Tertullian, *De praescr.* 6,37.

[27] Cf. Tertullian, *Adv. Marc.* 1,21; 4,5.

[28] Augustinus, *De bapt.* 4,31: "*Quod universa tenet ecclesia, nec conciliis institutum sed semper retentum est nonnisi auctoritate apostolica traditum rectissime creditur.*"

[29] Cf. for instance Rufinus, *Expositio Symboli apostolorum*, n. 2; CCL 20,134f.

[30] FC Ep 1, BC 464.

[31] DV 7.

tolic preaching, which is expressed in a special way in the inspired books" must be "preserved by a continuous succession of preachers until the end of time."[32] Though Lutherans and Catholics think differently in many respects about the way in which the apostolic norm is safeguarded, the shared conviction nevertheless is that "apostolicity" is an essential attribute of the church and the criterion par excellence of its faith, its proclamation, its teaching and its life.

(47) In the Lutheran-Roman Catholic dialogue to date this common conviction that the apostolic witness is the normative origin of the church has repeatedly been expressed and confirmed: The church stands for all time on the foundation of the apostles; it is in "all historical changes in its proclamation and structures ... at all times referred back to its apostolic origin."[33]

[32] DV 8.
[33] Malta Report, 57; cf. *The Ministry in the Church*, Roman Catholic/Lutheran Joint Commission, Geneva, 1982, 60, in *Growth in Agreement*, 248-275.

3. The Church of the Triune God

3.1 The Trinitarian Dimension of the Church

(48) It is our common confession that the church is rooted in God's election of Israel as well as being founded in the Christ-event and the proclamation of the gospel by the apostles in the Holy Spirit. So long, however, as this confession does not recognize the profound relationship of the church to God as Holy Trinity it remains inadequate and open to misunderstandings. This relationship of the church to the triune God is both causal and substantive, involving the differentiated yet reciprocal unity of Father, Son and Holy Spirit.

(49) The church is the communion of believers called into existence by the triune God. As such it is a divinely created human reality. That the church is anchored in the divine life of the triune God does not thereby negate its human dimension nor open the way to ecclesial presumptuousness. But it does preclude an understanding of the church which tends to regard it merely or even primarily as a human societal phenomenon. God allows the church to share in the triune divine life: the church is God's own people, the body of the risen Christ himself, the temple of the Holy Spirit (3.2). The church's unity or communion (*koinonia, communio*) partakes of and reflects the unity of the triune God (3.3).

(50) This biblical view of the substantive relation of the church to the triune God, which is developed in what follows, was profoundly familiar to the ancient church. It is alive in the more recent Roman Catholic understanding of the church, as is shown for instance by Vatican II's Dogmatic Constitution on the Church,[34] and the Orthodox-Roman Catholic dialogue.[35] But this trinitarian view is also at home in the Reformation view of the church. The Catholic-

---

[34] LG, especially 1.

[35] "The Mystery of the Church and of the Eucharist in the Light of the Mystery of the Holy Trinity," Joint International Commission for Theological Dialogue between the Roman Catholic Church and the Orthodox Church, 1982, especially II,1 and I,5/d.

Lutheran dialogue to date has repeatedly shown this[36] as has the statement of the Lutheran World Federation Assembly in 1984, "The Unity We Seek": the church and its unity "participates in the unity of the Father, Son and Holy Spirit."[37]

3.2 The Church as God's Pilgrim People, Body of Christ and Temple of the Holy Spirit

3.2.1 The Church as God's Pilgrim People

(51) When the church of the New Testament applies to itself the honorific title of Israel, "people of God," it is not using merely comparative language, nor is it simply referring to the sum of individual believers. Neither does "people of God" mean only that it is God who summons and holds this "people" together. Besides all these things it means that this people has its "holiness" and its fundamental character as a "chosen race" of God the Father by really belonging to God (1 Pet 2:9; cf. Ex 19:5f). As such, this "people," in its historical-terrestrial existence, is by no means immune to temptation, error, and sin. It is the "pilgrim" people of God standing under God's judgment for the duration of its earthly pilgrimage and depending upon God's daily renewal of grace and fidelity. Therefore it needs confession of sin and constant renewal. Nevertheless and precisely because of this, it is and remains the people who belong to God the Father.

(52) Since the coming of Jesus Christ the community of those who have been baptized in his name, who confess Christ and call upon him, has been the chosen people of God, a title hitherto applied only to the people of Israel. Two things are therein expressed simultaneously: the church's continuity with Israel and the dawn of a new stage of salvation history in which faith in the one God takes

---

[36] Cf. *Ways to Community*, Roman Catholic/Lutheran Joint Commission, Geneva 1981, 9-13, in *Growth in Agreement*, 215-240; *The Ministry in the Church*, 12; *Facing Unity*, Models, Forms and Phases of Catholic-Lutheran Church Fellowship, Roman Catholic/Lutheran Joint Commission, Geneva, 1985, 3, 88-90.

[37] *LWF Report* No. 19/20, 1985, 175.

shape as faith in the triune God and the community of God's elect expands to include believers in Christ from all peoples. The invitation to Israel remains open to join the chorus of faith in God's eschatological saving action in the proclamation, passion and resurrection of Jesus, the Messiah and the Son of God, and thus to belong to the communion of the church. In the picture of the Old Covenant pilgrim people of God, the church may recognize itself as the people of the New Covenant moving towards entry into the kingdom of God, the aim of its earthly pilgrimage. "People of God" thus expresses the intimate relationship of the church with Israel and of Israel with the church in the history of salvation.

(53) People from all nations belong together as Christians in the one universal church. As the people of God in the midst of all peoples, the church embraces all the diversity of the human world. It lives in many places and hears God's call in many languages and in a multiplicity of ways. Nevertheless it is a single undivided people, called by the one Lord, in one Spirit, to one faith, to solidarity and mutual love, to common witness and service in the world, and to be for people of all races and social classes. Thus in its being and its mission the church is a sign for the future unity of humanity.

(54) Through baptism the people of God is called to be a priestly people: "But you are a chosen race, a royal priesthood, a holy nation, God's own people, in order that you may proclaim the mighty acts of him who called you out of darkness into his marvelous light" (1 Pet 2:9). In both the Lutheran and the Catholic traditions, therefore, we rightly speak of the "priesthood of all the baptized" or the "priesthood of all believers."[38] What constitutes this priesthood is that all the baptized have access to God through Christ, the "one mediator" (1 Tim 2:5) and "high priest" (Heb 4:14), that all confess their faith in the one Lord, call upon him in prayer, serve him with their whole life and witness to all people everywhere (cf. 1 Pet 3:15).[39]

---

[38] Cf. WA 16,407; 38,247; LG 9-17; in the ecumenical dialogue cf. BEM, Ministry 1-6 in *Growth in Agreement,* 465-503; *The Ministry in the Church,* 12-13; *Kirchengemeinschaft,* 61.
[39] See below 5.1.

(55) Within the church as people of the New Covenant all social, racial and sexual divisions have in principle been overcome (cf. Gal 3:26-28). There are no privileges nor any precedence of some over the others (cf. Mt 23:8; Mk 9:35). In the world with its struggles for power, racial conflicts and social tensions, Christians are therefore in duty bound together with all people of good will, to contribute to reconciliation and peace. Like their Lord they are to care for the poor and the oppressed, to seek fellowship with them and to intervene publicly on their behalf. As witnesses to their Lord who is "the resurrection and the life" (Jn 11:25) Christians should everywhere be a light of hope for all "who have no hope" (1 Thess 4:13).

3.2.2 The Church as Body of Christ

(56) Also the New Testament references to the church as a "body" go far beyond the limits of a mere comparison. As a result of baptism all Christians become one body in the one faith through the one Spirit. The many members of that body do indeed have different tasks but they are nonetheless "individually ... members one of another" (Rom 12:4-5). This social reality of the church as a spiritual organism (cf. 1 Cor 12:14-26) has its actual basis in the sacramental reality of real participation in Christ and the linking of the lives of all Christian believers in and with Christ, the crucified and risen Lord: "Do you not know that all of us who have been baptized into Christ Jesus were baptized into his death? Therefore we have been buried with him by baptism into death, so that, just as Christ was raised from the dead by the glory of the Father, so we too might walk in newness of life" (Rom 6:3f). Consequently all are together not only "one body" (1 Cor 12:12) but also "the body of Christ" (1 Cor 12:27). Christ himself "is the head ... from whom the whole body, joined and knit together by every ligament ... promotes the body's growth in building itself up in love" (Eph 4:15f). Thus baptism is the entry into the Christian life in the sense of participation in Christ himself. It is the abiding foundation of all life and of all common life in the church.

(57) Rooted in baptism, this reality of the church as "Christ's body" finds ever new expression in the Lord's Supper. When the

Lord says: "This is my body that is for you" (1 Cor 11:24), the broken bread becomes for us all a "sharing in the body of Christ. Because there is one bread, we who are many are one body, for we all partake of the one bread" (1 Cor 10:16f). The designation of the church as "body of Christ" indicates, therefore, the elementary and vital bond between Christ, the Lord's Supper and the church: "Baptized by the one Spirit into the one body (cf. 1 Cor 12:13) believers — nourished by the body of Christ — become ever more one body through the Holy Spirit."[40] Christ who is himself really present in the celebration of the Lord's Supper, "nourishes and tenderly cares for" his church as his body (Eph 5:29f), after making "her holy by cleansing her with the washing of water by the word" (Eph 5:26). Just as in anticipation the people in the wilderness "all ate the same spiritual food and all drank the same spiritual drink ... Christ" (1 Cor 10:3f), so the church lives through its Lord, present in the Holy Supper as the "bread of life" (Jn 6:35), "the living bread that came down from heaven" so that the promise holds: "Whoever eats of this bread will live forever" (Jn 6:51). "Those who eat my flesh and drink my blood have eternal life ... [they] abide in me, and I in them" (Jn 6:54-56).

(58) It is from this sacramental reality of the church as "Christ's body" that the spiritual-diaconal reality of its common life flows. As Paul describes it, all Christians are equipped and called by God's Spirit to fulfill the membership given to them in the body of Christ in a distinctive way (cf. 1 Cor 12:4-6; Rom 12:6-8). Each one is needed and all need each other (cf. 1 Cor 12:14ff.). "Like good stewards of the manifold grace of God, serve one another with whatever gift each of you has received" (1 Pet 4:10; cf. Eph 4:7). All are to serve "the building up" of the church and its unity (Eph 4:12) with their gifts and are to contribute to peace (cf. Eph 4:3), which means concretely "for the common good" of all (1 Cor 12:7). Thus the principle of all living together in the church is love (cf. 1 Cor 13:13-14:1). This finds expression in the structures of the Church's life.

[40] *The Eucharist*, Lutheran/Roman Catholic Joint Commission, Geneva, 1980, 25, in *Growth in Agreement*, 190-214.

3.2.3 The Church as Temple of the Holy Spirit

(59) Reference to the constitutive relation between church and Holy Spirit runs through the whole New Testament witness concerning the church. Here too the question is not only that of a causal relation — in the sense that the Holy Spirit makes the church of the New Covenant come into existence, that the proclamation of the gospel takes place in the power of the Spirit, that it is the Spirit who awakens faith in those who hear the gospel, and that the Spirit bestows on the church his manifold gifts. The Holy Spirit does all that by remaining in the church and entering into a close and substantive relation with the church. It is part of the mystery of the church that the Spirit of God is its spirit. This finds expression in the image of the church as "temple of the Holy Spirit." Even if the direct application of this concept to the church is not found in the New Testament, it is nevertheless quite clear that the New Testament statements regarding the Holy Spirit and his relation to the church have this intention.

(60) The Holy Spirit is "poured out" on the disciples and on all who accept the message of Christ in faith (Acts 2:17f.; 10:45); the Spirit is "distributed"[41] (Heb 2:4) and "given" (e.g. 2 Cor 1:22; Eph 1:17) and they "receive" (e.g. Acts 1:8; 2:38; 1 Cor 2:12; Gal 3:14) and "have" (Rom 8:9) the Spirit. Believers are "filled" with the Holy Spirit (e.g. Acts 2:4; 9:17; Eph 5:18), so that they are now in "the spirit" and live, walk and serve (e.g. 1 Cor 14:16; Gal 5:16; 5:25; 1 Pet 4:6) "in" the Spirit — i.e., "in the new life of the Spirit" (Rom 7:6). So it can then be said that the Holy Spirit "dwells" (1 Cor 3:16; Jas 4:5) in the believers and that they are "the temple of the living God" (2 Cor 6:16; cf. 1 Cor 3:16), "a temple of the Holy Spirit" (1 Cor 6:19).

(61) That which is true of believers as individuals is also true of the community of believers as a whole, the church: they are to be "built together spiritually into a dwelling place for God" (Eph 2:22), into a "spiritual house" (1 Pet 2:5), and they are to grow "into a holy temple in the Lord" (Eph 2:21). The greeting and the blessing of the Apostle is

---

[41] "*merismós pneúmatos agioû.*"

40

addressed to the community as a whole: "the communion of the Holy Spirit be with all of you" (2 Cor 13:13). This Holy Spirit, with whom the community has "communion" and who dwells in the church as in a holy temple, leads men and women to faith by the proclamation of the gospel (cf. 1 Thess 1:5), acts in baptism (cf. Acts 2:38; 1 Cor 6:11), and in the Lord's Supper (cf. 1 Cor 10:1-4; 12:13) for their salvation, supports them in their prayer (cf. Rom 8:26), and through Christ gives them access to God the Father (cf. Rom 8:14-16; Eph 2:18). The Spirit strengthens the witnesses of the gospel (cf. 1 Thess 1:5-7), maintains the church in truth (cf. Jn 14:26), and bestows upon it the manifold riches of his gifts (cf. 1 Cor 12:4-6). The one Spirit is the principle of the church's unity (cf. 1 Cor 12:13; Eph 4:3f). As God's power, through which Jesus was raised from the dead (cf. Rom 1:4), the Spirit is, amidst the earthly life of the church, the "first installment" of the future fullness of salvation (2 Cor 1:22), in which the faithful already participate and which is the goal of their earthly pilgrimage.

(62) Catholics and Lutherans both teach that the church as a community of believers is called and gathered together by the Holy Spirit through the proclamation of the gospel in word and sacrament, and is empowered by the Holy Spirit who works in and through it. The statements contained in Luther's Small and Large Catechisms[42] here coincide with those of the Dogmatic Constitution on the Church[43] of Vatican II.

3.3   The Church as *Koinonia/Communio* Founded in the Trinity

3.3.1   The Unity of the Church Sustained and Formed by the Triune God

(63) Participation in the communion of the three divine persons is constitutive for the being and life of the church as expressed in the

---

[42] Cf. BC 345, 415-420.
[43] Cf. LG 4.

three New Testament descriptions of it as "people of God," "body of Christ" and "temple of the Holy Spirit." Thus the church also shares in the communion of the Father with the Son and of both with the Holy Spirit. The unity of the church as communion of the faithful has its roots in the trinitarian communion itself, as this is expressed in the greeting of the first letter of John: "...so that you also may have fellowship with us; and truly our fellowship is with the Father and with his Son Jesus Christ" (1 Jn 1:3; cf. Jn 17:21).

(64) This can already be seen in the fact that the three designations of the church are not simply interchangeable, while being intimately linked together and refering to each other. This corresponds to the inseparable but at the same time differentiated unity of the three divine persons and their activity.

— The church as "people of God" of the New Covenant is the communion of those who have been baptized in Christ's name and have received the Holy Spirit.
— As "body of Christ," the faithful and the church have a share in Christ who was raised from the dead "by the glory of the Father" (Rom 6:3f); and through the Holy Spirit the faithful are incorporated into the body of Christ, and they receive their gifts for the building up of the body.
— In the church as "temple of the Holy Spirit" it is the Spirit who as "the Spirit of Christ" (Rom 8:9; cf. 2 Cor 3:17) binds the faithful to Christ, the mediator of all salvific gifts, and who through him gives them access to the Father, whom they may invoke as "Abba, Father" in the same Spirit.

(65) However one looks at the church, whether as "people of God" or "body of Christ" or "temple of the Holy Spirit," it is rooted in the inseparable communion or *koinonia* of the three divine persons and is thereby itself constituted as *koinonia*. It is not primarily the communion of believers with each other which makes the church *koinonia*; it is primarily and fundamentally the communion of believers with God, the triune God whose innermost being is *koinonia*. And yet the communion of believers with the triune God is inseparable from their communion with each other.

3.3.2 *Koinonia/Communio* through Preaching, Baptism and the Lord's Supper

(66) That the church as *koinonia* is based in the trinitarian *koinonia* is shown and realized in the proclamation of the gospel, baptism and the Lord's Supper.

(67) The preaching of the gospel, from which the church as fellowship of believers lives, can be rightly understood only in its trinitarian frame of reference. But it also links the individual believer and all believers with God in the divine trinitarian *koinonia*. The church's preaching proclaims the "good news of Christ" (Rom 15:19; cf. 1:16). In their preaching the apostles and with them all witnesses to the gospel are "ambassadors for Christ" (2 Cor 5:20). They "teach" what Jesus Christ — who will remain with them "always, to the end of the age" — has "commanded" them (Mt 28:20). The preaching of the gospel of Christ takes place in the "power" of the "Holy Spirit" (Acts 1:8). The Spirit calls and empowers the witnesses for their ministry (cf. Jn 20:22f; 2 Cor 4:13). The Spirit awakens and sustains the faith which accepts the gospel that is preached as the promise of salvation (cf. 1 Thess 1:5f: 1 Tim 1:14) and which responds to it in confession (cf. 1 Cor 12:3). In this proclamation by the apostles and all the witnesses — a proclamation which is sustained by the Holy Spirit — Jesus' preaching of the "good news of the kingdom of God," by which he called people to him and gathered them around him, is continued after Easter and Pentecost. Jesus' preaching in word and deed acquired its authority solely from the fact that his words and deeds were identical with those of the Father who had sent him (cf. Jn 14:10 and 24; Jn 8:28; 10:15). Of Jesus as "beloved" Son of the Father can it be said, "listen to him!" (Mt 17:5; par).

(68) Baptism in the name of the Father, Son and Holy Spirit (Mt 28:19) leads us into communion with the triune God and into sharing in his blessings and thus also knits believers together into a communion. Baptism is calling and election by God and makes us God's possession: thus also creating the community of those who are called and chosen, "God's own people" (1 Pet 2:9). In baptism we are

baptized into Christ's body, partaking of his death and resurrection, and putting on Christ: consequently the baptized also constitute "one body ... one with another" (Rom 12:4f) and are one communion in which creaturely and social divisions no longer count for anything (cf. Gal 3:26-28). The baptized receive the Holy Spirit: they are thus also bound together into one communion "in the one Spirit" (1 Cor. 12:12f; Eph 4:3f).

(69) The celebration of the Lord's Supper draws believers into the presence and communion of the triune God through thanksgiving (*eucharistia*) to the Father, remembrance (*anamnesis*) of Christ and invocation (*epiklesis*) of the Holy Spirit. In a special way the celebration is the *koinonia* of believers with the crucified and risen Lord present in the Supper, and for that very reason it also creates and strengthens the *koinonia* of the faithful among and with each other. Paul says: "The cup of blessing that we bless, is it not a sharing in the blood of Christ? The bread that we break, is it not a sharing in the body of Christ? Because there is one bread, we who are many are one body, for we all partake of the one bread" (1 Cor 10:16f). His rebuke of the Corinthians follows this dialectic precisely; when their practice of the the Lord's Supper violates their *koinonia*, they profane their eucharistic communion with the Lord (cf. 1 Cor 11:20-29).

(70) It is the common conviction of our churches that in and through the eucharistic *koinonia* with Christ ecclesial *koinonia* is established and strengthened. On the Catholic side one can point for instance to Vatican II, especially to its Dogmatic Constitution on the Church[44] or to Thomas Aquinas for whom the reality (*res*) of the Lord's Supper is "the mystical body of Christ" in which we are strengthened "through unity with Christ and with his members."[45] On the Lutheran side this conviction is expressed for instance in Luther's sermon on "The Blessed Sacrament of the Holy and True Body of Christ and the Brotherhoods 1519"[46] which is important for his ecclesiology, or in Martin Chemnitz's commentary on 1 Cor 10 in which, adopting the trinitarian standpoint, he says, "In the Lord's

[44] E.g. LG 7; cf. LG 3.
[45] Thomas Aquinas, *Summa Theologiae* III,73a.1; 79a.5.
[46] WA 2, 742-758; LW 35,45-73.

Supper ... we all receive one and the same body of Christ ... and because in this way the members of the church are fused into one body of Christ, they are also bound up with each other and become one body whose head Christ is. Thus when we receive the body and blood of Christ in the Lord's Supper, we are closely bound up with Christ ... and through Christ we are united with the Father... Thus we become partakers (*koinonoi*) of the Father, the Son and the Holy Spirit. This all comes about from the saving communion (*koinonia*) of the body and blood of the Lord ..." [47]

(71) In these explanations based on the New Testament witness, both our traditions understand themselves to be in agreement with the ancient church for which the Pauline statements on *koinonia* in Christ were decisive. St. John of Damascus summarizes this patristic theological tradition as follows: "If [the eucharist] is also called communion, and truly is so, because of our having communion through it with Christ and partaking both of His flesh and His divinity, and because through it we have communion with and are united to one another. For, since we partake of one bread, we all become one body of Christ and one blood and members of one another and are accounted of the same body with Christ." [48]

3.3.3 *Koinonia/Communio* as Anticipatory Reality

(72) The three biblical designations of the church as "people of God," "body of Christ" and "temple of the Holy Spirit" all interpret its trinitarian basis in anticipatory fashion:

— The universal people of God will first gather in its entirety on the last day; only in anticipation of that ultimate gathering can the church be the people of God today who live already on the basis of what God will make of them.

---

[47] Martin Chemnitz, "*Fundamenta sanae doctrinae de vera et substantiali praesentia ... corporis et sanguinis Domini in Coena*," IX.

[48] Saint John of Damascus, *The Orthodox Faith* IV,13, *The Fathers of the Church*, Vol. 37, Washington, 1958, 361.

— The church is the body of the crucified and risen Christ for whose return in glory we still wait.

— The church is the temple of the Holy Spirit whose reality among us is "down payment" (*arrabón*) of eschatological reality.

Thus the church is already everything the biblical designations of it say it is — but in such a way that it awaits in anticipation, what is most profoundly its being and the source of its life.

(73) This also holds good for the church as *koinonia*. It is already a partaking in the *koinonia* of the Father, Son and Holy Spirit; but as the pilgrim church it is such provisionally and in fragmentary fashion; and this means in anticipation and expectation of its final destination, which is still pending: consummation in the kingdom of God, in which the triune God will be "all in all" (1 Cor 15:24-28).

3.4   Ecclesial Communion — Communion of Churches

3.4.1   Common Witness

(74) On both the Catholic and the Lutheran side the concept of *koinonia/communio* has once more become important ecclesiologically, indeed it has become central. In Lutheranism this becomes clear in the increasing use, and above all theological deepening, of the term "church fellowship/communion" which it has been possible to observe more or less since the 1950s. The term is understood as an acceptance of the concept of *koinonia/communio* in the early New Testament church as described above, and it can also claim the support of the Reformation view of the church and incorporate specific aspects of it. Especially since Vatican II the idea of *koinonia/communio* and the term itself have become determinative for the Catholic view of the church. In this we see "the central and fundamental idea" of the ecclesiology developed by the Council. [49]

[49] Documents of the Extraordinary Synod, The Final Report, Rome, 1985, in *The Tablet*, 14 December 1985, II,C,1.

(75) On the basis of a concept of *koinonia* derived from the New Testament and the early church, Lutherans and Catholics agree that the church is a *koinonia/communio* rooted in the mystery of the holy Trinity. Proof of that assertion is found both in the Lutheran Confessions and documents of Vatican II.

(76) According to the teaching of the Council "human dignity lies in man's call to communion with God."[50] The Council refers to 1 John 1:2f, according to which believers are to attain *koinonia* with the Father and the Son, for God has revealed himself so that "through Christ ... man has access to the Father in the Holy Spirit and comes to share in the divine nature."[51] God thus seeks "to establish peace or communion between sinful human beings and Himself, as well as to fashion them into a fraternal community."[52] In this way the mystery of the church is indicated, for according to the Council the communion with God in the body of Christ effected through the Holy Spirit is the foundation for the *koinonia* of the church. The Spirit dwells in the faithful, guiding and governing the church. It establishes the "communion of the faithful and joins them together ... in Christ."[53]

(77) The Lutheran Confessions indicate the chief meaning of church fellowship by designating the nature of the church as the communion of the faithful[54] which originates in communion with Christ through the Holy Spirit, and which lives from faithful hearing of the word and receiving of the sacraments. When CA 7 describes the "one holy Christian church" as the "assembly of all believers,"[55] it means that "communion of saints"[56] of which the Apostles Creed speaks.[57] The fact that "communio" is understood and translated as "assembly" or "congregation" and not, for linguistic reasons,

---

[50] GS 19.
[51] DV 2.
[52] AG 3.
[53] UR 2.
[54] *Communio/congregatio sanctorum/fidelium.*
[55] CA 7, BC 32.
[56] *Communio sanctorum.*
[57] Apol 7,8; BC 169; cf. translation and interpretation of *communio sanctorum* in Luther's Large Catechism as "a communion of saints," as "a little holy flock or community;" BC 416f.

rendered "community" in German, should not cause the term to lose any of its New Testament or early church content or meaning. There is no sociological reductionism involved. Instead the fellowship (*communio*) is an assembly or congregation "under one head, Christ, called together by the Holy Spirit," in which "I also am a part and member, a participant and co-partner in all the blessings [*Güter*] it possesses. I was brought to it by the Holy Spirit and incorporated into it through the fact that I have heard and still hear God's Word, which is the first step in entering it."[58] "To have communion or fellowship" therefore does not simply mean "having some relationship with another person" but rather that "many persons share or eat or partake of one common thing."[59] Just as the communion of Christians with each other is grounded in their common sharing in Christ, so it is for them a communion of mutual sharing and mutual help and service: "This fellowship is twofold: on the one hand we partake of Christ and all saints; on the other hand we permit all Christians to be partakers of us, in whatever way they and we are able."[60]

(78) According to the Second Vatican Council, it is through the word of preaching and the celebration of the sacraments, of which the eucharist is the "center and summit," that Christ the author of our salvation becomes present in the church.[61] "From the table of both the word of God and of the body of Christ" the "bread of life" is offered to the faithful.[62] In the breaking of the eucharistic bread they actually gain a share in the Lord's body and are raised to communion with him and among one another, for communion in the body of Christ makes those who receive the one bread into the body of the Lord.[63] The eucharist is therefore the summit of ecclesial *communio*[64] and "the very heartbeat of the congregation of the faithful."[65]

---

[58] LC II,3; BC 417; cf. Apol 7,8: "'Church' means, namely, the assembly of saints who share the association of the same Gospel or teaching and of the same Holy Spirit, who renews, consecrates, and governs their hearts." BC 169.

[59] Luther to the term *koinonia* in 1 Cor 10,16ff; WA 26,493; LW 37,356.

[60] WA 2,754; LW 35,67.

[61] AG 9.

[62] DV 21.

[63] Cf. LG 7 with reference to 1 Cor 10:16f; cf. LG 3.

[64] Cf. LG 11.

[65] PO 5: "*congregatio fidelium.*"

(79) Catholics and Lutherans together understand that the communion with God mediated through word and sacrament leads to communion of the faithful among themselves. This takes concrete shape in the communion of the churches: the one holy catholic and apostolic church, the *una sancta* of the creed, is realized in the *communio ecclesiarum* as local, regional and universal communion, and so as church fellowship.

(80) There is only one church of God. In the New Testament the same word *ecclesia* signifies both the whole church (e.g. Mt 16:18; Gal 1:13) and the church of a region (e.g. Gal 1:2), the church of a city (e.g. Acts 8:1; 1 Cor 11:18) or of a house (e.g. Rom 16:5). Accordingly, Lutherans and Catholics see the church of God in local, regional and universal terms, but these different ways in which the church becomes a reality must be understood on the basis of the one holy catholic and apostolic church, the *una sancta* of the Creed.

(81) Because the church, as communion of the faithful, is based in communion with Christ, the one Lord, there is only one single church. According to the Lutheran Confessions the promise that it will "remain forever" applies only to that *una sancta ecclesia*. [66] That church is "a holy Christian people," [67] persons "scattered throughout the world who agree on the Gospel and have the same Christ, the same Holy Spirit, and the same sacraments." [68] The church "is mainly an association of faith and of the Holy Spirit in men's hearts." [69]

(82) According to the Second Vatican Council, "God has gathered together as one all those who in faith look upon Jesus as the author of salvation and the source of unity and peace, and has established them as the Church, that for each and all she may be the visible sacrament of this saving unity. While she transcends all limits of time and of race, the Church is destined to extend to all regions of the earth, and so to enter into the history of mankind." [70] "The Church, then, God's only flock,

[66] CA 7; BC 32; cf. Apol 7,9; BC 169f.
[67] LC II,3; BC 417.
[68] Apol 7,10; BC 170.
[69] Apol 7,5; BC 169.
[70] LG 9.

like a standard lifted high for the nations to see, ministers the gospel of peace to all mankind, as she makes her pilgrim way in hope toward her goal, the fatherland above."[71]

(83) Looked at diachronically — through all time — the *una sancta* as an eschatological reality pervades the whole of history, from the first days (*ecclesia ab Abel*) to the last, the time of Christ's return in glory. It has taken shape especially since the elect people of God has become the body of Christ and the temple of the Holy Spirit and hence represents for the faithful the place of new life and of that communion with God which finds expression in communion with each other.

3.4.2   The Lutheran Understanding of Local Church

(84) Differences between the Catholic and Lutheran positions appear when the question is posed about the realization of the church from a synchronic — here and now — point of view. For Lutherans the local congregation is church in the full sense; for Catholics it is the local church led by its bishop.

(85) Lutherans understand the *una sancta ecclesia* to find outward and visible expression wherever people assemble around the gospel proclaimed in sermon and sacrament. Assembled for worship the local congregation therefore is to be seen, according to the Lutheran view, as the visible church, *communio sanctorum*, in the full sense. Nothing is missing which makes a human assembly church: the preached word and the sacramental gifts through which the faithful participate in Christ through the Holy Spirit, but also the ministers who preach the word and administer the sacraments in obedience to Christ and on his behalf, thus leading the congregation.

(86) The understanding of the church as communion of persons based on communion with the one Lord includes the communion of separate congregations bound together in true communion with Christ. Therefore congregations may not distance themselves nor

---

[71] UR 2.

isolate themselves from one another. The communion they have in Christ must be visible.

(87) Lutheran congregations are part of larger fellowships which are themselves constitutionally structured. According to geographical, historical, national or political realities they form dioceses or juridically autonomous provincial or national churches. These larger communities are held together by communion in Christ, and that shows itself in their common understanding of the apostolic faith (confessional communion), in word and sacrament (pulpit and altar fellowship), and in a mutually recognized ministry.

(88) In the second half of the 19th century consciousness of the global dimension of ecclesial communion grew stronger among the Lutheran churches. First came regional[72] and finally world-wide Lutheran associations.[73] For decades the Lutheran World Federation understood itself as "free association of churches" — having common confessions but without having declared pulpit and altar fellowship. The concept of "church fellowship" played an increasingly important role as the Federation responded to repeated questions about its ecclesial character. "Church fellowship" combined the New Testament/patristic concept of *koinonia/communio* with the Lutheran understanding of church.[74] More recently it was the concept of communion itself which became the *leitmotif* of efforts toward the clarification and new definition of the nature of the Lutheran World Federation, efforts which came to their conclusion in the decision of the Federation's 1990 Assembly. Now the constitution states: "The Lutheran World Federation is a communion of churches which confess the triune God, agree in the proclamation of the Word of God and are united in pulpit and altar fellowship."[75]

(89) It therefore becomes clear what, according to Lutheran understanding of the church as *koinonia*, is constitutive, irrespective of whether the expression is congregational, territorial/national or

---

[72] North America and Europe.
[73] Lutheran World Convention 1923; Lutheran World Federation 1947.
[74] CA 7.
[75] LWF Constitution III: Nature and Functions.

global: the common understanding and confession of the apostolic faith (confessional communion) and communion in preaching and the sacraments (pulpit and altar fellowship), including by implication the ministry of proclamation and the administration of the sacraments (recognition of ministries).

(90) This understanding of church as *koinonia* was and is determinative for ecumenical efforts of the Lutheran churches. The sought for visible unity of the church is, in this sense, understood as ecclesial communion. [76] The statement of the 1984 Lutheran World Federation Assembly, "The Unity We Seek," is developed by explicit use of the concept of communion. [77]

3.4.3. The Roman Catholic Understanding of Local Church

(91) When Catholics view the church synchronically and spatially, they understand that it expresses itself throughout the earth as local church, regional church and universal church, but that none of these expressions can be exclusively identified with the *una sancta*. Rather the *una sancta* is for each expression the criterion for unity in the truth. [78]

---

[76] Cf. *Agreement between Reformation Churches in Europe (Leuenberg Agreement)*, 1973, Frankfurt, 1993, 29 and 33; *Facing Unity*, 23-26.

[77] *LWF Report* No. 19/20, Budapest 1984, 175.

[78] The terminology for describing the local church and the church as a whole (all the local churches that are in communion with each other) does not derive from a systematic and critical decision. Even Vatican II did not come to such a decision. Consequently in the Council's documents, *ecclesia localis* and *ecclesia particularis* can desginate the diocesan church, but with equal frequency the two terms also describe associations of diocesan churches. *Ecclesia universa* (used on twenty-three occasions) and *ecclesia universalis* (used on twenty-five occasions) designates the church as a whole or the universal church. This is never described as the Church of Rome.

The *Codex Iuris Canonici* of 1983, which does not have the expressions *ecclesia localis* and *ecclesia universalis*, makes use of the two terms *ecclesia particularis* (diocese) and *ecclesia universa* (the church as a whole). Catholic theologians have not wholly identified themselves with this choice of terms. They prefer to reserve the term "particular church" (*ecclesia particularis*) for associations of churches which are characterized by their special cultural features, and to describe the church in one place as the "local church" in order to preserve the catholicity of the church.

In German this leads to preferring the term *Ortskirche* ("local church") to "particular church" and likewise to the term "partial church" (which suggests the false idea that the local church is a part of the universal church).

(92) In Catholic ecclesiology the local church is essentially neither a part of the universal church nor an administrative or canonical district of it. According to the teaching several times stated at Vatican II, the church of God is truly present and effective in the local church, i.e., diocese.[79] The decree on the Bishops' Pastoral Office states, "A diocese is that portion of God's people which is entrusted to a bishop to be shepherded by him with the cooperation of the presbytery. Adhering thus to its pastor and gathered together by him in the Holy Spirit through the gospel and the Eucharist, this portion constitutes a particular church in which the one, holy catholic, and apostolic Church of Christ is truly present and operative."[80] The theology of the local church here presented coheres with the conciliar theology of the people of God.[81] The expression "portion" (*portio*) was deliberately preferred to "part" (*pars*) because a "portion" contains all the essential features of the whole — which is not the case with "part." In other words the local church has all the qualities of the church of God and one must not therefore look upon it as a branch office of the universal church. The mention of the bishop points to the structural fellowship of the local churches with each other, for as a result of his ordination the bishop functions as a connecting link of the church, both as the representative of the whole church in his church, and as the representative of his church in relation to all the others.[82] The reference to the presbytery points to the collegial nature of the ministry in the local church.

(93) On the level of the diocese one finds a full presence of the church of God. Moving out from this level, the fundamental conciliarity of the church is expressed in the participation of the bishop in a council. Since however parishes also have the structural characteristics of the church of God ("portion" of the people of God, Holy Spirit, gospel, eucharist and ministry), the Second Vatican Council recognizes: "parishes set up locally under a pastor who takes the place of the bishop ... in a certain way represent the visible Church as it is established throughout the world."[83] In actual fact it is the parish,

[79] Cf. SC 41; LG 23 and 26; CD 11.
[80] CD 11.
[81] Cf. LG, chapters 2 and 3.
[82] Cf. LG 23 and *Facing Unity*, 112.
[83] SC 42.

even more than the diocese, which is familiar to Christians as the place where the church is to be experienced.

(94) Each of the constitutive elements of the local church ("portion" of the people of God, Holy Spirit, gospel and eucharist, presidency of the bishop) and their presence together show that the local church is indeed the church of God in the full sense, but that it cannot be regarded as the whole church of God. "The local church is not a free-standing, self-sufficient reality. As part of a network of communion, the local church maintains its reality as church by relating to other local churches."[84] Part of its nature is to be in real fellowship with other local churches and with the church as a whole.

(95) This fellowship of the local church with the church universal is not an abstract, purely theoretical reality. In the local church one encounters the essential mystery of the church: in the local church one is instructed in the faith and led to a confession of the Apostolic Faith, and only there can one be baptized, confirmed, ordained, married and receive the Lord's body at his table. Only through the local church is one a member of the Catholic Church. Nor can one conceive of the universal church apart from the local churches, as if the whole church could exist apart from the local churches. In actuality, "in and from such individual churches there comes into being the one and only Catholic Church."[85] In both terms — "in these" and "out of them" — the reciprocal nature of the relationship is expressed, not the priority of one over the other. If "out of them" is deleted, the universal church would desintegrate into separate particular churches; if one removes "in these," the local church is degraded into nothing but an administrative unit of the universal church.

(96) The relation of "reciprocal inherence"[86] or "mutual indwelling"[87] which exists between the local and the universal church neither

[84] The Church: Local and Universal, 36, Joint Working Group between the Roman Catholic Church and the World Council of Churches, Geneva-Rome, 1990.

[85] LG 23.

[86] International Commission of Theologians: Themata Selecta de Ecclesiologia (Documenta 13). Vaticano 1985, 32: "mutua interioritas."

[87] John Paul II, Speech to the Roman Curia, 20 December 1990, AAS 83 (1991), 745-747.

dissolves the independence of the local church nor its essential inclusion in the universal church but consolidates both, in the same way as the ultimate responsibility of each bishop to God for his local church and for his faithful does not call in question his inclusion in the college of bishops with the pope. According to the teaching of the Council the bishop is the "visible source and foundation" for the unity of the local church and the "Roman Pontiff ... is the visible source and foundation of the unity of the bishops and of the multitude of the faithful," while the local churches are fashioned after the model of the universal Church. [88] Thus the church is a unity in and out of diversity, it is a body of churches, [89] or a *communio* of churches.

(97) The fellowship of local churches, that is to say the church universal, is therefore not a platonic entity. It is what supports each individual church. Only for the church universal does the promise hold good of remaining in the truth. That cannot be said of any local church. In periods of great crisis where the specific expression of faith was at stake, only the fellowship of all the churches, and especially the ecumenical councils, succeeded in working out answers in spite of all the well-known communication difficulties. The contributions and initiatives which single local churches made toward resolving disputed questions had their full impact only in the framework of reception by the communion of churches. Generally it is true that "mutual solicitude, support, recognition, and communication are essential qualities among local churches. Even from earliest times, the local churches felt themselves linked to one another. This *koinonia* was expressed in a variety of ways: exchange of confessions of faith; letters of communion as a kind of 'ecclesiastical passport'; hospitality; reciprocal visits; mutual material help; councils; and synods." [90]

(98) A consequence of the universal character of the great commission in the New Testament (cf. Mt 28:19; Acts 1:8: 2:1-12) is the pluriformity of the local churches within the church catholic. It is also

---

[88] LG 23.
[89] *Corpus ecclesiarum* (LG 23). The reason of the corporeality of the church is the sacramental sharing in the body of Christ; see above 76 and 78.
[90] *The Church: Local and Universal*, 37.

a matter of experience that effective evangelization has been possible only through the formation of regional churches strong enough to influence a whole culture. An image in the Decree on the Church's Missionary Activity of Vatican II makes it plain how the universality of mission calls for the involvement of human cultures in the faith and thus requires as well the specific characteristics of the particular churches as conditioned by their cultural context: it is the church which after Pentecost "speaks all tongues, which lovingly understands and accepts all tongues, and thus overcomes the divisiveness of Babel."[91] This church is entrusted with a universal yet unique message. Consequently it must avoid the danger of particularism, that is, it must be ready to understand and respect as valid the language of the other. At the same time, the church's missionary task is to follow Christ who committed himself "in virtue of His Incarnation, to the definite social and cultural conditions of those human beings among whom He dwelt."[92] In this sense the "congregation of the faithful, endowed with the riches of its own nation's culture, should be deeply rooted in the people."[93]

99. Thus the particular churches are catholic in the full sense only if they have gone through a process of critical inculturation which requires them, within the culture and society in which they live, to examine what has to be affirmed, purified, and integrated.[94] In "each major socio-cultural area" the emergence of particular churches pre-supposes that "every appearance of syncretism" be excluded and that "particular traditions, together with the individual patrimony of each family of nations, can be illuminated by the light of the gospel, and then be taken up into Catholic unity. Finally, the individual young Churches, adorned with their own traditions, will have their own place in the ecclesiastical communion ..."[95] Thus the catholicity of the whole church will be enriched by the catholicity of the particular churches. Accordingly, the Dogmatic Constitution on the Church sketches this ideal: "in virtue of this catholicity each individual part of

[91] AG 4.
[92] AG 10.
[93] AG 15.
[94] Cf. LG 13.
[95] AG 22.

the Church contributes through its special gifts to the good of the other parts and of the whole Church. Thus through the common sharing of gifts and through the common effort to attain fullness in unity, the whole and each of the parts receive increase."[96]

(100) As a result of taking seriously the special character of particular churches Vatican II also hopes for a stimulus for the restoration of unity among the separated Christians. The Constitution on the Church states that "this variety of local churches with one common aspiration is particularly splendid evidence of the catholicity of the undivided Church,"[97] and the Decree on Ecumenism says: "Let all members of the Church, according to the office entrusted to each, preserve a proper freedom in the various forms of spiritual life and discipline, in the variety of liturgical rites, and even in the theological elaborations of revealed truth. In all things let charity be exercised. If the faithful are true to this course of action, they will be giving ever richer expression to the authentic catholicity of the Church, and, at the same time, to her apostolicity."[98]

(101) Because cultural units are usually more comprehensive than a diocese, it is necessary that this definition of particular churches be actualized by associations of local churches, for example in the classical form of patriarchates, or in the modern form of churches *sui iuris* and by conferences of bishops of the same or several nations, or on the level of a whole continent, e.g. CELAM.[99] One must further note patriarchal, provincial, and plenary synods as well as the declarations of the bishops' conferences. It is also the task of the papal Primate to protect proper diversity. "Moreover, within the Church particular Churches hold a rightful place. These Churches retain their own traditions without in any way lessening the primacy of the Chair of Peter. This Chair presides over the whole assembly of charity and

---

[96] LG 13.
[97] LG 23.
[98] UR 4.
[99] Consejo Episcopal Latinoamericano (Council of Latin American Bishops).

protects legitimate differences, while at the same time it sees that such differences do not hinder unity but rather contribute toward it."[100]

(102) The gospel of salvation is directed to the whole of humanity: God created the church with a view to universal reconciliation and unity, and Jesus promised to remain with his church to the end of the age (cf. Mt 16:18; 18:20; 28:20; Eph 4:1-13). In this sense the *una sancta* and the church universal will always have precedence over the local churches. At the same time it is true that the church of God has always assumed a local shape; for Christians receive baptism, celebrate the eucharist and give a socially identifiable witness always in a particular place. In this sense there will always be a priority of the local churches over the church as a whole, but not over the eschatological *una sancta*. Consequently we may speak of a reciprocity in the relations between the local and the universal church. But it is different with the *una sancta* which permeates the whole of history as an eschatological reality and with which no realization of the church of God as a local, regional or universal church can be exclusively identified.

(103) The eucharist best expresses the reciprocal relation between the local churches, the universal church and the eschatological church. "Since Pentecost the church celebrates the eucharist as the one, holy, catholic and apostolic church. The eucharistic celebration, therefore, embraces the church both in its local and universal dimension. It thus affirms a mutual presence of all the churches in Christ and in the Spirit for the salvation of the world."[101]

(104) In the documents of Vatican II the designation "mother church" is not applied to any local church nor even to the Church of Rome, but is strictly reserved for the *una sancta*. This demonstrates that the fellowship of all the churches makes them sisters in its bosom. As the Decree on Ecumenism puts it, there is that "communion of faith and charity ... which ought to thrive between local Churches, as between sisters."[102]

[100] LG 13.
[101] *The Church: Local and Universal*, 24.
[102] UR 14; cf. *Facing Unity*, 44f.

3.4.4 Tasks of Further Dialogue

(105) The Catholic view of the church as *koinonia/communio* may be made fruitful for ecumenical endeavor, [103] and it too — like the Lutheran view of a "church fellowship" — has its specific emphases and configurations. However, the fundamental idea in both cases is the same and is ecclesiologically determinative in the same way. It is part of the nature of every local church to be open towards the other local churches. Catholicity requires that.

(106) According to the belief of the Catholic Church, of course, the primatial function of the bishop of Rome is an essential element of the church, with the consequence that each local church must be related to the primacy of the Church of Rome and its bishop in order to be in the full communion of churches. But on the other hand it must not be forgotten that the Roman primacy is also related to the *koinonia* of the local churches. The Catholic-Lutheran dialogue must deal with the question of the ministry of oversight in the whole church in the context of ecclesial *koinonia* in general, but also in the particular context of the Roman Catholic understanding of the relationship between the episcopal college and the papal office. To be sure a problem thereby arises in regard to the Catholic ecclesiology of communion to which the ecumenical dialogue has, in various ways, called attention. In spite of Catholic adherence to the principle of a ministry of unity in the universal church, the challenge to self-criticism cannot be ignored. The doctrine of primacy must be further developed, and primatial practice must be shaped accordingly. One hopes, therefore, that in its further work the Catholic-Lutheran dialogue on ecclesiology will take up the theme of a ministry of leadership for the universal church within the framework of communion ecclesiology.

---

[103] Cf. *Facing Unity*, 5-7.

4.   The Church as Recipient and Mediator of Salvation

(107) In the summary of the biblical witness on the abiding origin of the church it was stressed that the proclamation of the gospel by the apostles in the Holy Spirit is the foundation of the church, and that as *creatura evangelii* the church is committed to serving the gospel. [104] Thus the church is the recipient and mediator of salvation. In the great biblical images of the people of God, the body of Christ and the temple of the Holy Spirit, the church shows itself to be a *koinonia* founded in the life of the triune God from whom it receives life and salvation, and the church imparts life and salvation in faithfulness to its task of mission, which it has received from God. [105]

4.1   The Church as *Congregatio Fidelium*

(108) A comparison of Lutheran and Catholic views of the church cannot disregard the fact that there are two fundamentally inseparable aspects of being church: on the one hand the church is the place of God's saving activity (the church as an assembly, as the recipient of salvation) and on the other it is God's instrument (the church as ambassador, as mediator of salvation). But it is one and the same church which we speak of as the recipient and mediator of salvation. In the course of the history of theology the emphases have been variously placed. While Lutherans see the church mainly as the recipient of salvation, as the "congregation of the faithful," *congregatio fidelium*, contemporary Catholic theology emphasizes more the church as the mediator of salvation, as "sacrament" of salvation. [106]

---

[104] See above 2.4.
[105] See above 3.3.
[106] See below 4.2.

4.1.1 The Lutheran View

(109) "The Creed calls the holy Christian church a *communio sanctorum,* 'a communion of saints'."[107] Luther thus repeats in the Large Catechism what he had already set out in *A Brief Explanation ... of the Creed:* "I believe that there is on earth, through the whole wide world, no more than one holy, common Christian Church, which is nothing else than the congregation, or assembly of the saints, i.e., the pious, believing men on earth, which is gathered, preserved, and ruled by the Holy Ghost, and daily increased by means of the sacraments of the Word of God."[108] Thus the church is not simply the sum of its individual members, for it is founded on the very word of God that faith receives, and individuals belong to it by receiving the word and sacrament in faith. The power of the Holy Spirit is what produces and sustains this assembly of believers among whom the individual is reckoned.

(110) According to the Augsburg Confession the church is "the assembly of all believers among whom the Gospel is preached in its purity and the holy sacraments are administered according to the Gospel."[109] The Apology explains this: "the church is ... mainly[110] an association of faith and of the Holy Spirit in men's hearts. To make it recognizable, this association has outward marks, the pure teaching of the Gospel[111] and the administration of the sacraments in harmony with the Gospel of Christ."[112] The context makes clear that "pure doctrine and conformity to the gospel" indicates the message of justification by which the church's life must be evaluated and to which the church as a whole is subordinated. In this the Augsburg Confession restates the teaching of the ancient, but also the medieval church. [113] The church receives its whole life and being from Christ, whose body it is, and who "renews, consecrates and governs [it] by his

---

[107] LC III,47; BC 416.
[108] WA 7,219; LW Phil.Ed. II,373.
[109] CA 7 (and 8); BC 32; BSLK 61,1: *"Congregatio sanctorum [et vere credentium], in qua evangelium pure docetur et recte administrantur sacramenta."*
[110] *principaliter,* cf. CA 8: *proprie.*
[111] *pura evangelii doctrina.*
[112] Apol. 7,5; BC 169.
[113] Cf. CA 1 and 3.

Spirit."[114] It can live only on the basis of this promise of the forgiveness of sins and the fellowship of salvation which has been bestowed on it. The church is gift in every respect because it lives by the Spirit of God and from the Lord present in it.

(111) The proclamation of the gospel and the celebration of the sacraments characterize the church as communion of salvation where Christ is present and where we can find him: "Those who are to find Christ must first find the church ... But the church is not wood and stone but the mass of people who believe in Christ; one must hold to it and see how they believe and pray and teach; they assuredly have Christ with them."[115] Luther emphasizes the necessity of the church for the salvation of individuals so strongly that he can say, "I believe that no one can be saved who is not found in this congregation, holding with it to one faith, word, sacraments, hope and love."[116] Similarly the church is highlighted in the Apology as the place of the promise of salvation for children. They are to be baptized, so that they will share Christ's promise, which "does not apply to those who are outside of Christ's church, where there is neither Word nor sacrament, because Christ regenerates through Word and sacrament."[117] "For the kingdom of Christ is only where the Word of God and the sacraments are to be found."[118] Faith and listening to the voice of the good shepherd, Jesus Christ, distinguish the church as God's people from every other people; for, "thank God, a seven-year-old child knows what the church is, namely, holy believers and sheep who hear the voice of their Shepherd."[119] The church is therefore the *congregatio fidelium*, the congregation of salvation as a faith-congregation, founded by God's word and bound to it: "God's Word cannot be present without God's people, and God's people cannot be without God's Word."[120]

114 Apol 7,5; BC 169.
115 WA 10,I/1:140,8.14.
116 WA 7,219,6; LW Phil.Ed. II,373.
117 Apol 9,2; BC 178.
118 Ibid., German text.
119 SA III,12; BC 315.
120 WA 50,629,34; LW Phil.Ed. II, 271.

(112) Faith in the gospel allows believers to place their salvation entirely in God's hands and makes them free to serve God and humanity. The gift of the faith-community becomes the task of acting in line with *koinonia;* everything is common to everyone in the congregation of salvation. Luther says: "I believe that in this congregation or Church, all things are common [cf. Acts 2:44], that everyone's possessions belong to the others and no one has anything of his own; therefore, all the prayers and good works of the whole congregation must help, assist and strengthen me and every believer at all times, in life and death, and thus each bear the other's burden, as St. Paul teaches" (cf. Gal. 6:2). [121] The "communion of believers," *communio credentium*, finds concrete expression in the general priesthood of all believers. By baptism all believers receive a share in the priesthood of Christ. They can and should therefore witness to the gospel and intercede for each other before God. "Therefore because he [a Christian] is a priest and we are his brothers, all Christians have power and authority and must so act that they preach, and come before God each asking for the other and offering themselves up to God." [122] In the general priesthood a representational authority is given; for one is always a priest for others. Understood in this way, being a Christian is a social *charisma*, a service before God for and to others.

4.1.2 The Catholic View

(113) *Congregatio fidelium* was the predominant definition for the church in the late medieval theology. The *Catechism of the Council of Trent* (*Catechismus Romanus*) too speaks of the church as "the congregation of the faithful." [123] To it belong all "who were called by faith to the light of truth and the knowledge of God, that … they may worship the living and true God piously and holily, and serve him from their whole heart." [124] The Catechism also refers to Augustine's words with regard to Psalm 140: "The Church … consists

[121] WA 7,219,11; LW Phil.Ed. II, 373.
[122] WA 12,308,4.
[123] *Catechism of the Council of Trent* I,10,2; *Cat. Rom.* I,10,5: *"coetus omnium fidelium."*
[124] *Ibid.* I,10,2.

of the faithful people, dispersed throughout the world." [125] In reference to the Apostles Creed, the Catechism sees a statement about the church [126] in the words, "communion of saints." [127] As communion on the basis of the confession of faith and the sacraments as well as the communion of life, this "communion of saints" is described as mutual love and mutual helping in sorrow and need. For this view the Catechism has recourse above all to the Pauline statements on the church as the body of Christ; the gifts of God are given for the use of the whole church and should benefit everyone. [128]

(114) The church is the assembly of those who believe in Christ. Vatican II describes the whole church as "all those, who in faith look upon Jesus as the author of salvation" [129] and calls the individual congregation the "congregation of the faithful;" [130] it thus appropriates the terminology of Augustine, who describes the church as redeemed community, [131] the "community and society of the saints." [132] *Communio* is the fundamental ecclesiological concept of the Council even if it uses the idea of *communio* on many levels and nowhere defines it. The church was established by Christ as "fellowship of life, charity and truth" [133] and the Holy Spirit "gives her a unity of fellowship and service." [134] The entire saving work of Jesus Christ and therefore the church is founded in the mystery of the triune God; "in order to establish peace or communion between sinful human beings and Himself, as well as to fashion them into a fraternal community, God determined to intervene in human history in a way both new and definitive." [135] This communion with God and of human beings among themselves is brought about by God's word and the sacraments. "For those who believe in Christ, who are reborn not from a perishable but from an imperishable seed through the Word of the living God (cf. 1 Pet

[125] *Ibid.*
[126] *Ibid.* I,10,24.
[127] *Communio sanctorum.*
[128] *Catechism of the Council of Trent* I,10,23-27.
[129] LG 9.
[130] AG 15; 19; PO 4f.
[131] *Civitas redempta.*
[132] PO 2.
[133] LG 9.
[134] LG 4: *in communione et ministratione.*
[135] AG 3.

1:23), not from flesh but from water and the Holy Spirit (cf. Jn 3:5-6), are finally established as 'a chosen race, a royal priesthood'... (1 Pet 2:9-10)."[136] The Council states that in Christ "all the faithful are made a holy and royal priesthood. They offer spiritual sacrifices to God through Jesus Christ, and they proclaim the perfections of Him who has called them out of darkness into His marvelous light. Hence, there is no member who does not have a part in the mission of the whole Body."[137] The Council calls this priesthood the "common priesthood"[138] to distinguish it from the "ministerial priesthood."[139] The eucharist is pre-eminent among the sacraments; "the Eucharistic Action is the very heartbeat of the congregation of the faithful over which the priest presides."[140] "Truly partaking of the body of the Lord in the breaking of the Eucharistic bread, we are taken up into communion with Him and with one another."[141]

(115) The Council states equally clearly that "the People of God finds its unity first of all through the Word of the living God ... For through the saving Word the spark of faith is struck in the hearts of unbelievers, and fed in the hearts of the faithful."[142] The proclamation of the word is essential for the right administration of the sacraments; "for these are sacraments of faith, and faith is born of the Word and nourished by it."[143]

(116) The Decree on the Church's Missionary Activity describes pointedly the power of God's word to justify and awaken faith: "The Holy Spirit, who calls all men to Christ by the seeds of the word and by the preaching of the gospel, stirs up in their hearts the obedience of faith. When in the womb of the baptismal font He begets to a new life those who believe in Christ, He gathers them into the one People of God."[144] Nor is the judging power of God's word in any way ignored.

---

[136] LG 9.
[137] PO 2.
[138] LG 10.
[139] Ibid.
[140] PO 5.
[141] LG 7 referring to 1 Cor 10:17.
[142] PO 4.
[143] Ibid.
[144] AG 15.

"The words of Christ are at one and the same time words of judgment and grace, of death and life. For it is only by putting to death what is old that we are able to come to a newness of life. … By himself and by his own power, no one is freed from sin or raised above himself, or completely rid of his sickness or his solitude or his servitude. On the contrary all stand in need of Christ, their Model, their Mentor, their Liberator, their Savior, their Source of life." [145] Thus the church lives as a communion of believers, not by its own strength but entirely from God's gift. This of course becomes its task in passing on the faith and mediating salvation.

4.1.3 Common Witness

(117) Both Lutherans and Catholics understand the church as the assembly of the faithful or saints which lives from God's word and the sacraments. Seen thus, the church is the fruit of God's saving activity, the community of his truth, his life and his love. Christ who acts in his saving word and sacrament, confronts the church which is the recipient of his and the Holy Spirit's activity. The presence of Christ marks the church as the place where salvation takes place. The gift of salvation however becomes the task and mission of the church as the community which has received salvation. Thus the church is taken by its Lord into the ministry of mediating salvation. That holds good in association and mutual support within the congregation of the faithful itself but also particularly in confronting the world, especially all who still do not believe and still do not belong to the assembly of the faithful.

4.2   The Church as "Sacrament" of Salvation

4.2.1   The Church under the Gospel
and the Twofold Salvific Mediation of the Gospel

(118) The Lutheran-Roman Catholic dialogue has stated that the church "stands under the gospel and has the gospel as its superordi-

---

[145] AG 8.

nate criterion."[146] For this one can appeal both to Luther, who sees the church as "creature of the gospel"[147] and to Vatican II according to which "the gospel ... is for all time the source of all life for the Church."[148] The gospel by which the church was created and lives is mediated externally and corporally in dual form: by word and by sacrament. Both modes of mediation however are connected in fundamentally indissoluble fashion without doing away with their specific characteristics. The word proclaimed is an audible sign, the sacraments are a visible word. These are the two modes in which the transmission of the gospel is saving in its effect. Thus not only is attention drawn to salvation or information given about it, but the gospel thus confronts people in their inmost selves as effectual externally and corporally by its presence, bringing them to faith, justifying and sanctifying them.

(119) Because in this way the church lives from the gospel and is taken into the service of the dual mediation of the gospel that effects salvation, Catholic talk of the church as "sacrament" can be described in terms of its purpose: "as the body of Christ and *koinonia* of the Holy Spirit, the church is the sign and instrument of God's grace, an instrument that of itself can do nothing. The church lives by the word as it lives by the sacraments and at the same time stands in their service."[149] The meaning of what is said about the church as the "sacrament" of salvation will be worked out below with reference to the Catholic and Lutheran traditions and their common foundation in the Bible.

4.2.2   The Catholic View

(120) In the documents of Vatican II the church is referred to as "sacrament" — a sign and instrument of salvation — especially where the nature of the church and its universal mission are explained in considerable detail. At the beginning of the Constitution on the

---

[146] Malta Report, 48.
[147] WA 2,430,6: *creatura ... Evangelii.*
[148] LG 20.
[149] *Facing Unity*, 85.

Church there is a programmatic statement "Christ is the light of all nations."[150] By the church's proclamation of the gospel to all creatures (cf. Mk 16:15) all people are to be illumined by the radiance of Christ which "brightens the countenance of the Church;" for "by her relationship with Christ, the Church is a kind of sacrament of intimate union with God, and of the unity of all mankind, that is, she is a sign and an instrument of such union and unity."[151] The Council underlines very distinctly the Church as centered in Christ, when it sees its "sacramentality" to be completely "in Christ." Catholic theology therefore speaks also of the "primal sacrament" (*Ursakrament*) which Jesus Christ himself is. The Council takes this direction when it speaks in the Constitution on the Sacred Liturgy of the "Mediator between God and man: ... For His humanity, united with the person of the Word, was the instrument of our salvation. Thus in Christ 'there came forth the perfect satisfaction needed for our reconciliation, and we received the means for giving worthy worship to God'."[152]

(121) Of the church as the "messianic people" we also read: "Established by Christ as a fellowship of life, charity, and truth, it is also used by Him as an instrument for the redemption of all, and is sent forth into the whole world as the light of the world and the salt of the earth (cf. Mt 5:13-16)."[153] The Council sees the establishment of the church as rooted in the whole mystery of Christ[154] but links the statement of the church as "sacrament" in a special way with the resurrection of Christ and the sending of the Spirit: "Rising from the dead (cf. Rom 6:9), He sent His life-giving Spirit upon His disciples and through this Spirit has established his body, the Church, as the universal sacrament of salvation. Sitting at the right hand of the Father, He is continually active in the world, leading men to the Church, and through her joining them more closely to Himself ..."[155]

---

[150] LG 1.
[151] *Ibid.*
[152] SC 5.
[153] LG 9.
[154] Cf. LG 2-5.
[155] LG 48; cf. LG 7; 59.

(122) The term "sacrament," as a sign and instrument of salvation, gives expression to the universal mission of the church and its radical dependence on Christ. It thus becomes clear that neither the foundation of the church nor its goal lies in the church itself and that it therefore does not exist by itself or for itself. Only in and through Christ, only in and through the Holy Spirit is the church effectual as a mediator of salvation. That is especially important when theologians speak of the sacraments as self-actualizations of the church, in order to prevent a purely outward understanding of the church as simply the steward of sacraments as means of grace, and instead to set forth an inner affinity, which though is not an identity, between the church and the sacraments, both being signs and instruments of salvation. As a "communion of life, love and truth" on the one hand and as an "instrument for the salvation of everyone" and as "universal sacrament of salvation" on the other hand, the church is the actual place and instrument of the universal saving will of God "who desires everyone to be saved and to come to the knowledge of the truth" (1 Tim 2:4). God's will that all should be saved becomes for the individual a gracious promise when the church testifies to the truth of Christ and celebrates and proffers the sacraments, i.e., when Christ's salvation is present in the witness and sacramental celebration of the church done in and through Christ and thus in and through the Holy Spirit. In the church — his body and his bride — Christ himself remains thus present for all people of the world through his saving acts.

(123) In Catholic thought the concept of "sacrament" is constantly applied to the church analogically. [156] Church is not "sacrament" in the same sense as the sacraments of baptism and the eucharist. That is already clear in reference to how they function: the individual sacraments develop their saving efficacy "on the basis of their being celebrated;" [157] their efficacy is not dependent on the worthiness of the minister or the recipient because it is Christ who

---

[156] Thus the term "sacrament" is always placed within quotation marks when related to the church in order to draw attention to the analogous use of language. This is expressly highlighted in the Dogmatic Constitution on the Church when talking of the church as "a kind of [veluti] sacrament ... a sign and an instrument ..." (LG 1).

[157] ex opere operato.

effects salvation in the sacraments. That cannot be said about the church as "sacrament" in the same way. Rather, one applies the concept of sacrament to the church to aid in theological reflection, for it clarifies the inner connection between outward, visible structure and hidden, spiritual reality. Just as the sacraments in scholastic thinking are described as visible signs and instruments of invisible grace, so Vatican II sees the church as "one interlocked reality which is comprised of a divine and a human element" in which "the communal structure of the Church serves Christ's Spirit, who vivifies it by way of building up the body (cf. Eph 4:16)." [158] But this view of the church as "sacrament" also stands in the context of the effective imparting of salvation to all people: "The one Mediator ... communicates truth and grace to all" through the church. [159] Speaking of the church as "sacrament" in the context of salvation for all people and of mission theology shows especially that Vatican II did not simply take over such earlier theories as "primal sacrament." Rather, the Council's own theological point of departure is a further development of earlier considerations.

(124) Here again we see that although it is his body, the church cannot be simply identified with Christ absolutely. It is taken into his service to mediate salvation to all people and needs the constant vivifying power of the Holy Spirit. In influencing its own members it is Christ who as head grants participation in his Spirit and who thus causes the life and growth of the body. [160] It is part of the logic of such a sacramental concept of the church that the church in its human weakness must "incessantly pursue the path of penance and renewal" [161] and be called to "continual reformation." [162] Even outside the "visible structure" of the church "many elements of sanctification and of truth can be found" [163] and God's saving activity is visibly and latently at work at the same time among "those who have not yet received the gospel." [164]

[158] LG 8.
[159] *Ibid.*
[160] Cf. LG 7 referring to 1 Cor 12, Eph 1 and Col 2.
[161] LG 8; cf. 48.
[162] UR 6.
[163] LG 8; cf. UR 3f.
[164] LG 16; GS 22.

4.2.3 The Lutheran View

(125) For Lutheran theology it is of fundamental and crucial importance that God bestows forgiveness, life and the bliss of salvation on every believer through word and sacraments as means of grace[165] and that the church as the "assembly of all believers" is the place "in" which these means of grace are effectual.[166] This means that preaching as "the living voice of the gospel"[167] itself has "sacramental" character, given that within the audible word lies the power to impart to the faithful that reality of salvation to which the words of the proclamation point. "When I preach, Christ himself preaches in me."[168] Thus the "external word,"[169] as an "effectual word"[170] stands alongside the sacraments as means of grace. We "must constantly maintain that God will not deal with us except through his external Word and sacrament."[171] The teaching of the Anabaptists "that the Holy Spirit comes to us ... without the external word of the Gospel"[172] is therefore expressly condemned as such. The condemnation of the Donatists — for whom the sacraments become useless and ineffectual when administered by "wicked priests" — likewise points to the objective efficacy of word and sacrament, which remain "efficacious even if the priests who administer them are wicked men,"[173] because they are instituted and enjoined by Christ.

(126) But if the church is the place where these means of grace become effectual it follows that the church itself is in a derivative sense an instrument of salvation. On the one hand it is called into being as a *congregatio fidelium*, a church, through the event of the "means of grace" so that it is itself a *creatura evangelii*; on the other, it is the place where people participate in salvation — there is no

---

[165] Cf. CA 5.
[166] CA 7.
[167] *viva vox evangelii*.
[168] WA 20,350,6: "*Quando ego praedico, ipse [sc. Christus] praedicat in me.*"
[169] *verbum externum*.
[170] *verbum efficax*.
[171] SA III,8; BC 313.
[172] CA 5; BC 31.
[173] CA 8; BC 33.

alternative. In this sense it is true for Reformation theology too that there is no salvation outside the church. [174]

(127) As mediator of word and sacrament the church is the instrument through which the Holy Spirit sanctifies; "it is the mother that begets and bears every Christian through the Word of God," [175] but in such a way that Jesus Christ himself is working and becomes salvifically present in its preaching and administration of the sacraments. In other words, however much the mediating activity of the church and the saving activity of God coincide in what happens there, they are nevertheless plainly different in this: while it is true that the church imparts participation in salvation to believers, nevertheless it is Christ alone and not the church who has gained salvation for the world and who bestows on believers participation in this salvation through word and sacrament. In what it does, the church is totally the servant of Christ, its Lord, being called to this service and given authority for it by Christ, its Lord.

(128) Against this background, Lutherans note affinities but also questions regarding the new Catholic understanding of the church as "sacrament." Lutheran thought corresponds more closely to the designation of Jesus Christ as "sacrament" found in Augustine [176] and later Roman Catholic theology. Christ is the "single sacrament" [177] of God, because he himself is the means par excellence of salvation. The individual sacraments are means of salvation because through them Jesus Christ accomplishes salvation and thus establishes and preserves the church. This means that the church does not actualize its own existence in the sacraments; rather the church receives salvation and its very being from Christ and, only as recipient does it mediate salvation. In this perspective, the individual sacraments are linked with Christ as he faces the church. One should be reticent about language which blurs this distinction. Talk about the church actualizing itself in the sacraments is open to serious misunderstanding and is better avoided. Lutheran theology points to

[174] *extra ecclesiam nulla salus*; cf. Apol 9,2; BC 178.
[175] LC I,40ff; BC 416.
[176] Augustine, Ep. 187, CSEL 57,113.
[177] Cf. WA 6,501,37; 86,7f; LW Phil.Ed. II,177.

the fact that calling the church "sacrament" must be clearly distinguished from the way "sacrament" is applied to baptism and the Lord's Supper.

(129) The first Lutheran query entails a second: how does the understanding of the church as "sacrament" relate to that of the church as holy and sinful? Differently from baptism and the Lord's Supper which exist wholly in their instrumentality and sign-character, the church is instrument and sign of salvation as the community of those who receive salvation. In other words, the church is instrument and sign as the community of believers who as people justified by God are at the same time holy and sinful. Lutherans point out that Catholic references to the church as "sacrament" must not contradict the fact that the church is at the same time holy and sinful. [178]

(130) There are certainly Lutheran theologians who apply "sacrament" to the church. Yet reservations about references to the church as "sacrament" remain in Lutheran theology, since such references can lead to misunderstandings on both the points just explained. Therefore many confine themselves to speaking of the church as sign and instrument of salvation in the sense already outlined.

4.2.4 The Unity and Distinctness of Christ and the Church

(131) We can leave it to further theological reflections to determine how Christ and the church are one in sacramental activity without thereby being identified, and how a possible sacramental view of the church therefore has its roots in the fundamental description of Christ as the "primal sacrament" and is limited by that statement. Talk of the church as "sacrament" is in fact foreign to the Lutheran ecclesiological tradition and is acceptable only under the reservations just set forth — reservations which Catholic theologians also take seriously. Nevertheless, harking back to the biblical witness we can together state the following.

[178] See below 4.4.

(132) The New Testament sees the mystery of the relationship between Christ and the church in unity and diversity. The unity is highlighted in a series of statements, for instance when Paul not only sees baptized believers as "one in Christ" but addresses them as such (Gal 3:28). According to Paul, the community is "one body in Christ" (Rom 12:5), and as "body of Christ" (1 Cor 12:27) is in fact "Christ" (1 Cor 12:12). It becomes clear that this unity in Christ does not imply an undifferentiated identity when Christ is described as "head of the body, the church" (Col 1:18; cf. Eph 1:22f; 4:14ff; 5:23). We are to distinguish head from body but on no account to separate them, for the "building up [of] the body of Christ" (Eph 4:12-16) proceeds from Christ, the head, who has saved the church as his body (cf. Eph 5:23). "The church is subject to Christ" always (Eph 5:24) and linked to him in love (cf. Eph 4:16). The interlinking of unity and diversity becomes clear especially in the image of the bride and bridegroom (cf. 2 Cor 11:2; Eph 5:22ff; Rev 19:7f; 21:2; 22:17).

(133) Of course the personal relation between Christ and church must not obscure the different quality of relations between the two; for from the start the church is the redeemed, receiving church and remains so for ever. Precisely in the light of the doctrine of justification it becomes plain that the church owes its existence and activity solely to the mercy of God in Jesus Christ and to the breath of the Spirit. Only so is Christ able to make salvation effectual through the church in proclamation and the sacraments. Both the Lutheran and Catholic understandings of the church's salvific service through word and sacrament are based on this biblical foundation. We can leave it to theological reflection to explain in greater detail how this works, if only it becomes and remains clear that God's eschatological promise of grace really determines the church's activity and guides it from within, and that salvation thus appears palpably in history. Nevertheless it must be evident that salvation can never be effected by human beings or be at their disposal, but even in the activity of the church it remains the gift of God.

(134) On the basis of the stipulations mentioned, there is agreement among Lutherans and Catholics that the church is instrument and sign of salvation and, in this sense, "sacrament" of salvation. To be

sure the reservations are taken seriously by both sides, and one must strive for a theological language that is unambiguous.

4.3 The Church Visible and Hidden

(135) The view has often been advanced that the terms "visible church" and "invisible church" point to a disagreement between Roman Catholic and Lutheran ecclesiologies. Often one appeals to Luther's saying, the holy church "is invisible, dwelling in the Spirit, in an 'unapproachable' place."[179] Post-Reformation Catholic ecclesiology reacted polemically to such an understanding of the church, and focused almost exclusively on the church as an external, visible entity marked out by creed, sacramental structure and hierarchical leadership. Thus Bellarmine stressed that as an "association"[180] the church was "just as visible and palpable as the Republic of Venice."[181] In the nineteenth century especially, Lutherans and Catholics both thought that this was the essential difference in their ecclesiologies.

(136) But the assumed disagreement often lost its sharp contours, since each side repeatedly denied that it taught what the other side condemned. Thus Melanchthon in the Apology of the Augsburg Confession utterly rejected the reproach that the church was, in the Lutheran Reformation view, only a kind of "Platonic republic."[182] Nor — in the light of the pronouncements of Vatican II — can the reproach be sustained that the one holy church is equated undialectically on the Catholic side with its empirical historical form. For there it is said of the church that while "the visible assembly and the spiritual community" are indeed "not to be considered as two realities," they are nevertheless linked together asymmetrically: "... the communal structure of the Church serves Christ's Spirit, who vivifies it by way of building up the body (cf. Eph 4:16)."[183]

[179] WA 40/II,106,19; LW 27,84.
[180] *coetus.*
[181] Bellarmine, *Disputatio de conciliis et ecclesia*, III,ii.
[182] Apol 7,20; BC 171.
[183] LG 8.

(137) It seems that oversimplified formulations have led, wrongly, to the view that here the two churches are at odds. In what follows the aim is to examine whether there is ultimately a conflict between the two positions.

(138) On the Lutheran side the Augsburg Confession by no means describes the church as an invisible entity. Rather it describes the church as an "assembly"[184] to which a "ministry" constitutively belongs.[185] Also, regarding the words of Luther quoted above[186] one must note that they continue, "... therefore its [the Church's] holiness cannot be seen."[187] For Luther the word "church" here does not denote an invisible entity. His point is that the church does not display visibly the essential marks that qualify it as church — in this instance "holiness." That the word "church" nevertheless means a visible assembly becomes evident in the fact that there are "marks" of the church, "that is, Word, confession, and sacraments"[188] all of which represent extremely visible realities.

(139) The Lutheran view of the church is of course marked by a tension which may easily evoke misunderstanding of the "invisibility" of the church. According to the Apology, "hypocrites and evil men are ... members of the church according to the outward associations of the church's marks ... especially if they have not been excommunicated."[189] Thus it might seem as if there were on the one hand the invisible "association of the faith" and on the other the "outward association" which is recognizable by "marks." But Lutherans have rejected that view ever since the Apology.[190]

(140) Lutheranism sees the church as an "assembly." An assembly is not as such invisible. Invisible rather is the fact that this assembly really is church, i.e., that this visible body is the "body of Christ," that God really is at work in the word and in the sacraments

---

[184] CA 7; BC 32.
[185] CA 5 and 14; BC 31 & 36.
[186] See above 135.
[187] WA 40/II,106,20; LW 27,84.
[188] Apol 7,3; BC 169.
[189] *Ibid.*
[190] Apol 7,1-22; BC 168ff.

that are its visible marks and that its ministers are servants of the Holy Spirit. The predicate "invisible" is appropriate for the church in so far as it is an object of faith. This is also shown by the statement of Luther which has been quoted, in which he says "anyone who thinks this way turns the article of the Creed 'I believe a holy church' upside down; he replaces 'I believe' with 'I see'."[191] The same purpose is clearly revealed where Luther dissociates himself polemically from abuses of the ambiguous word "church" in ecclesiastical politics. "If these words had been used in the Creed: 'I believe that there is a holy Christian people,' it would have been easy to avoid all the misery that has come in with this blind, obscure word 'church'."[192]

(141) In the Lutheran view, certain aspects of the church's visibility are what it makes invisible: only to the eye of faith is an assembly recognizable as the assembly of the people of God, and yet — between the times — the church has to be visible. In this world what makes it a hidden church is the same as what made Christ on the cross a hidden God, i.e., that he was only all too visible in and for this world. The passage often quoted from Luther's Large Commentary on Galatians makes this clear. The crucial section reads: "God conceals and covers [the church] with weaknesses, sins, errors, and various offenses and forms of the cross in such a way that it is not evident to the senses anywhere."[193]

(142) The tension characteristic of the Lutheran understanding of the hiddenness of the church manifests a recurring problematic which all traditions have wrestled with in understanding the church and which they must continue to deal with. That is why Vatican II says that "possessing the Spirit of Christ" is fundamental to being "fully incorporated into the society of the Church." Those are not saved, however, who do "not persevere in charity," though they remain "indeed in the bosom of the Church" but "only in a 'bodily' manner and not 'in their hearts'."[194] In its Constitution on the Church, the Council does not solve the problem. The difficulty of the relationship

[191] WA 40/II,106,29; LW 27,85.
[192] WA 50.625,3; LW Phil.Ed. V,265.
[193] WA 40/II,106,21; LW 27,84; cf. Apol 7,19.
[194] LG 14.

between church membership "according to the heart" and membership only "according to the body," and thus between the church as spiritual and as visible corporeal entity is for us a common difficulty. To be sure, the Lutheran emphasis that the hiddenness of the church corresponds to a specific characteristic of the Christian faith, namely recognizing God at work in that which seems opposed to him, introduces a dimension which goes beyond the problem of the recognition of church membership.

(143) In statements quoted from Vatican II's Dogmatic Constitution on the Church, Lutherans discern important convergences in the way the church is understood. The Constitution sees the church unambiguously in the context of the mystery of the universal bestowal of the saving love of God the Father, as that is revealed in the history of Jesus as the Christ[195] and made effective by the Holy Spirit in election, reconciliation and communion, so that "all believers would have access to the Father through Christ in the one Spirit."[196] The Constitution resolutely maintains that the church is the "body of Christ." In so doing it follows the Pauline statements, but it avoids precise definition of membership in this body.[197]

(144) The Constitution on the Church produces a synthesis, which is new for Catholic theology, between the spiritual or transcendent reality of the church and its visible social reality. The spiritual community of faith, hope and love lives on the basis of the Father's gift. Through the one bread which Christ proffers, believers are made into one body, and as temple of the Holy Spirit the church is above all a mystery of communion with the triune God himself.[198] At the same time the church is also a historical reality. It began with Jesus' proclamation of the reign of God and the founding of the messianic people of the New Covenant, and this community of disciples has had unmistakable elements of social organization since the apostolic age.[199] The visible congregation stands in a complex relation to the

[195] LG 1-8.
[196] LG 4.
[197] Cf. LG 7.
[198] Cf. LG 8.
[199] Cf. LG 5; 9.

mystery of the *koinonia* in which it has its origin and to which it seeks to give credible shape. Because the Council posits an indissoluble link between the church as a visible assembly and the mystery of life shared in communion with God, it is possible to speak of the church as a "sacrament."[200]

(145) Crucial here is the analogy between the visible communal structure serving the life-giving Spirit, by which it is vivified, and the assumed human nature of Christ serving the Eternal Word.[201] By the very fact of its service, the social community is involved in a constant struggle as it journeys through history. Again and again it is in need of cleansing and renewal;[202] and this continuous reform encompasses all the moral, disciplinary and doctrinal witness of the church to God's grace.[203]

(146) A simple identification of the salvation-community with the empirical church, such as would place the empirical church beyond reform, is clearly labelled by Vatican II as an error which Catholic teaching should avoid.

(147) Catholics and Lutherans are in agreement that the saving activity of the triune God calls and sanctifies believers through audible and visible means of grace which are mediated in an audible and visible ecclesial community. They also agree that in this world the salvation-community of Christ is hidden, because as a spiritual work of God's it is unrecognizable by earthly standards, and because sin, which is also present in the church, makes ascertaining its membership uncertain.

4.4 Holy Church/Sinful Church

(148) With the creeds of the early church we confess in common that the church is "holy." This holiness essentially consists in the fact

[200] See above 4.2.
[201] Cf. LG 8.
[202] *Ibid.*
[203] Cf. UR 6.

that the church participates in the triune God, who alone is holy (cf. Rev 15:4), from whom it derives and to whom it is journeying:

— The church is holy through the gracious election and faithfulness of God. Just as the people of the Old Covenant were a "holy nation" because they had been chosen to be God's "treasured possession" (Ex 19:5f; cf. Lev 11:44f; Deut 7:6), so too by virtue of the new covenant of grace the church is God's "holy nation," the people who became his special possession (1 Pet 2:9).

— The church is holy through the saving work of Christ. Christ sanctified himself for his own, "so that they also may be sanctified in truth" (Jn 17:19); he sacrificed himself for the church, his "bride," "in order to make her holy" (Eph 5:25f).

— The church is holy through the presence of the Holy Spirit. The Holy Spirit dwells in believers as in a temple (cf. 1 Cor 3:16; 6:19; Eph 2:22); they are "sanctified by the Holy Spirit" (Rom 15:16; cf. 1 Cor 6:11); the Holy Spirit builds up the church and equips it by means of the gifts of the Spirit (cf. 1 Cor 12; Eph 4:11f); the Holy Spirit gives life to the church and strengthens it through spiritual fruits (cf. Gal 5:22).

(149) In so far as the holiness of the church continues to be rooted in the holiness of the triune God, we make common confession that the church in its holiness is indestructible. Christ has promised his presence to his disciples "to the end of the age" (Mt 28:20) and has promised his church that "the gates of Hades will not prevail against it" (Mt 16:18).

(150) Vatican II's Dogmatic Constitution on the Church states: "The Church ... is holy in a way which can never fail. For Christ, the Son of God, ... loved the Church as His Bride, delivering Himself up for her. This He did that He might sanctify her (cf. Eph 5:25-26). He united her to Himself as His own body and crowned her with the gift of the Holy Spirit, for God's glory." [204]

---

[204] LG 39.

(151) This belief in the indestructibility and abiding existence of the church as the one holy people of God is an essential element in Luther's ecclesiology and is fundamental for a correct understanding of his struggle for reform. "The Children's Creed [Catechism] teaches us (as was said) that a Christian holy people is to be and to remain on earth until the end of the world. This is an article of faith that cannot be terminated until that which it believes comes, as Christ promises, 'I am with you always, to the close of the age'."[205] In this sense the Augsburg Confession says, "It is also taught ... that one holy Christian church will be and remain forever."[206]

(152) This belief in the indestructibility of the one holy church includes the idea that in the ultimate sense the church cannot apostatize from the truth and fall into error. In this conviction the Reformation understands itself to be in continuity with the prior theological and ecclesiastical tradition; thus it has always understood the biblical promises in this way (cf. Mt 16:18; 28:20; Jn 16:13). So "the church cannot err"[207] repeatedly occurs in the Reformers in this or a similar form[208] and the Catholic-Lutheran dialogue has also referred to this shared conviction.[209]

(153) Of course the confession of the church's holiness has always gone hand in hand with the knowledge that the power of evil and sin, although it will not overcome the church, is nevertheless at work in it. The church "without a spot or wrinkle or anything of the kind" (Eph 5:27) will appear only at the end of its earthly pilgrimage, when "Christ will present her to Himself in all her glory."[210] The holiness of the church therefore exists both "already" and "not yet." It is a "genuine though imperfect holiness."[211]

(154) It is part of the theological tradition of our churches to apply the biblical pictures and parables of the weeds among the wheat

[205] WA 50,628,16; LW 41,148.
[206] CA 7; BC 32.
[207] *ecclesia non potest errare.*
[208] Cf. WA 18,649f; 30 III, 408; 51,513 and 515f; Apol 7,27; BC 173.
[209] E.g. Malta Report, 22f; *The Ministry in the Church*, 58.
[210] UR 4, cf. Augustine, *Retract.*, lib.II,c.18.
[211] LG 48.

(cf. Mt 13:38), the wise and foolish bridesmaids (cf. Mt 25:1ff) or the net and the fish (cf. Mt 13:47f), to the church in its visible and temporal reality: the church in its concrete form always includes good and evil people, believers and unbelievers, true and false teachers. The ancient church's condemnation of the Novatian and Donatist views of the church was adopted by the Reformation. The statement in Article 8 of the Augsburg Confession, that in the church, which is "properly speaking nothing else than the assembly of all believers and saints," there are nevertheless still "many false Christians, hypocrites and even open sinners ... among the godly,"[212] expresses a conviction shared equally by Catholics and Lutherans.

(155) As especially the Lutheran-Roman Catholic dialogue on justification has shown, there is also agreement that all believers as members of the church are involved in a relentless struggle against sin and are in need of daily repentance and the forgiveness of sins. They depend constantly on justifying grace and rely on the promise which is given them in the struggle against evil.

(156) With this in mind, it is not in dispute between us that the church is "holy" and "sinful" at the same time, and that the imperative calling to holiness is always a concomitant of the indicative that holiness has been bestowed (cf. 1 Thess 4:3f,7; 2 Cor 7:1). Thus the church is in constant need of repentance and the forgiveness of sins, and of cleansing and renewal. Vatican II stated this repeatedly, even if it does not use the term "sinful" of the church. The Dogmatic Constitution on the Church says: "While Christ, 'holy, innocent, undefiled' (Heb 7:26) knew nothing of sin (2 Cor 5:21), but came to expiate only the sins of the people (cf. Heb 2:17), the Church, embracing sinners in her bosom, is at the same time holy and always in need of being purified, and incessantly pursues the path of penance and renewal."[213] And the Decree on Ecumenism states, "Christ summons the Church, as she goes her pilgrim way, to that continual reformation of which she always has need, insofar as she is an institution of men here on earth."[214]

[212] CA 8; BC 33.
[213] LG 8; cf. 40.
[214] UR 6.

(157) Differences between our churches emerge in answering the question, Where does the idea of church's need for renewal or of its sinfulness find its necessary limit, by reason of the divine pledge that the church abides in the truth and that error and sin will not overcome it?

(158) The Lutheran Reformation no less emphatically than Roman Catholic theology stresses the fact that there is and must be such a limit. Thus Luther is able to distinguish between "erring" and "remaining in error." By this he wishes to show how abiding in the truth, which is promised to the church, is not a reality in peaceful possession, but, under the faithfulness and forgiveness of God, is realized in ongoing struggle against error.[215] Even more important is the distinction he makes between the teaching and the life of the church. Whereas in regard to its life the "holy church is not without sin, as it confesses in the Lord's Prayer 'Forgive us our sins',"[216] the opposite is true of its teaching, i.e., of its obedient proclamation of the gospel, insofar as the gospel is preached, the sacraments are administered and absolution is given "on behalf of Christ" (2 Cor 5:20)[217] and by his authority. "The teaching must be neither sinful nor reprehensible and it does not have its place in the Lord's Prayer in which we say 'Forgive us our sins.' For it is not our doing, but God's own Word which cannot sin or do wrong."[218]

(159) In this conception the Lutheran Reformation lies wholly in the realm of what is also maintained on the Catholic side. The conviction that the church's abiding in the truth — its indefectibility — is not a reality held in peaceful possession is also shared on the Catholic side. Therefore Catholics and Lutherans can say in common that "the church's abiding in the truth should not be understood in a static way but as a dynamic event which takes place with the aid of the Holy Spirit in ceaseless battle against error and sin in the church as well as in the world."[219] Luther's distinction between the life and

---

[215] WA 38,215f.
[216] WA 51,516,15.
[217] Cf. Apol 7:28; BC 173.
[218] WA 51,517,19; see also 513ff, especially 516f; cf. WA 38,216.
[219] Malta Report, 23.

the teaching of the church corresponds to the Catholic distinction between the "members" of the church, who in their constancy in faith, their life and their deeds are always in need of the forgiveness of sins and of renewal, [220] and the church itself, which in teaching and proclamation expounds the unalterable "deposit of faith;"[221] between the church as an "institution of men here on earth," which "Christ summons ... to ... continual reformation,"[222] and the church as "enriched with heavenly things," as a divine creation with the "elements of sanctification and of truth" given to it by Christ. [223]

(160) From the Lutheran standpoint serious questions to the Catholic view first present themselves where the God-given indestructible holiness of the church and God's promise that the church will abide in the truth are so objectivized in specific ecclesial components that they appear to be exempt from critical questioning. Above all this Lutheran query is directed at ecclesial offices and decisions which serve people's salvation and sanctification. The question arises when the Holy Spirit's aid is attributed to them in such a way that, as such, they appear to be immune from the human capacity for error and sinfulness, and therefore from needing to be examined. That will be dealt with in what follows. [224] Similar questions are also directed at the institution of the canonization of saints.

(161) These Lutheran questions cannot be regarded as superfluous, even in the light of the fact that in the Catholic view these ecclesial offices and decisions have their historically variable forms and are carried out by sinful human beings. For that reason they continue to be imperfect, can obscure the indestructible holiness of the church[225] and therefore are in need of reform. [226]

---

[220] Cf. LG 8; 40; DS 229 and 1537.
[221] UR 6.
[222] *Ibid.*
[223] LG 8; cf. UR 3.
[224] See 4.5.3.1-4.
[225] Cf. GS 43.
[226] Cf. UR 6.

(162) In fact these Lutheran queries touch directly on the self-understanding of the Roman Catholic Church at a decisive point; but they suggest conclusions which as such were not there from the beginning.

(163) The Lord's promise that it will abide in the truth is the basis for the Catholic Church's belief that the truth can be articulated in propositions and can lead to forms of expressing the gospel which are inerrant and infallible. [227] Further it believes that there are abiding, established ecclesial offices which are willed by God's providence. [228] Also that the saints perfected by God are not all anonymous, but are named, by canonization, as those who may be addressed as the perfected of God. [229]

(164) Thereby very diverse areas are addressed of which the first, inerrant truth, and the last, perfected holiness, have one thing in common: they express the fact that God's activity in this world — in its decisive and definitive quality — is incarnational and anticipates the eschaton. They of course represent such diverse levels that they should not simply be mentioned in one breath. Catholic thinking finds it hard to see why the effects of divine decisiveness should be intrinsically open to criticism and why it is not enough to distinguish between human sinfulness and the divine saving activity in such a way that, although they remain exposed to human inadequacy and sinfulness, God's works are inherently good and cannot be rendered ineffectual.

(165) In spite of the above questions one may, regarding the overarching problematic of the holiness of the church and its need for renewal, speak of common Lutheran-Roman Catholic basic convictions. Taken together they constitute a broad consensus within which remaining differences are neither abolished nor denied. Still only in discussing each of the relevant ecclesiological points in question is it possible to discover their theological and ecumenical importance.

[227] See below 4.5.3.3.
[228] See below 4.5.3.2
[229] See below 5.2.1.

4.5   The Significance of the Doctrine of Justification for the Understanding of the Church

4.5.1   The Problem and the Original Consensus

(166)   Many of the questions which Catholics and Lutherans address to one another regarding the relation between the doctrine of justification and the understanding of the church emerge from two different concerns, which may be summarized as follows: Catholics ask whether the Lutheran understanding of justification does not diminish the reality of the church; Lutherans ask whether the Catholic understanding of church does not obscure the gospel as the doctrine of justification explicates it. Neither concern is unfounded, but needs to be clarified, especially because the New Testament knows of no opposition between gospel and church.

(167) In dealing with the relationship between the doctrine of justification and the understanding of the church, it is important to note which perspective on justification is employed. It is not primarily a matter of how the saving event can be rightly described and how God communicates his righteousness to the sinner. This indeed stands at the center of Reformation arguments but, as such, has no immediate critical implications for ecclesiology. These emerge only when — as happened especially in the Lutheran Reformation — justification is seen both as center and criterion of all theology. Therefore the doctrine of the church must correspond to justification as criterion. The reciprocal questions of Catholics and Lutherans mentioned above arise only from such a perspective.

(168)   The far-reaching consensus in the understanding of justification noted during this and other Lutheran-Roman Catholic dialogues leads to testing the consensus on the critical significance of the doctrine of justification for all church doctrine, order and practice. Everything which is believed and taught regarding the nature of the church, the means of grace and the ordained ecclesial ministry must be grounded in the salvation-event itself and bear the mark of justification-faith as reception and appropriation of that event. Corre-

spondingly, all that is believed and taught regarding the nature and effects of justification must be understood in the total context of assertions about the church, the means of grace and the church's ordained ministry. Expressing the Lutheran position, the Malta Report of 1972, "The Gospel and the Church," stated: "... all traditions and institutions of the church are subject to the criterion which asks whether they are enablers of the proper proclamation of the gospel and do not obscure the unconditional character of the gift of salvation."[230] In the United States the Lutheran-Roman Catholic dialogue took over this assertion as its common declaration: "Catholics as well as Lutherans can acknowledge the need to test the practices, structures and theologies of the church by the extent to which they help or hinder 'the proclamation of God's free and merciful promises in Christ Jesus which can be rightly received only through faith'."[231]

4.5.2   Common Basic Convictions

(169) Just as the New Testament does not acknowledge a fundamental contradiction between gospel and church, so we too must beware lest we see justification and the church as being from the outset in conflict with each other, let alone as being incompatible. Three basic convictions, shared by Catholics and Lutherans, and which lead from the doctrine of justification into ecclesiology, prevent that.

(170) First, the gospel, as the Reformation doctrine of justification understands it, is essentially an "external word." That is to say it is always mediated through one or more individuals addressing one or more other individuals. The gospel is not a doctrine that can be internalized as one's own in such a way that thereafter no further address from other persons is needed. It remains a message "from outside" and hearers remain dependent on its communication by one who proclaims it. This is expressed, for instance, in Article 7 of the

---

[230] Malta Report, 29.
[231] *Justification by Faith*, 153; cf. 28.

Augsburg Confession, which describes the church not simply as the "assembly of all believers" or *congregatio sanctorum* but also links this "assembly of all believers" constitutively to the "external" witness of the gospel in preaching and the sacraments, which conversely can have their place only in the church, "the assembly of all believers." [232] On the one hand the church lives from the gospel; on the other the gospel sounds forth in the church and summons into the community of the church.

(171) Second, the gospel which is proclaimed in the Holy Spirit is according to its nature a creative word. If belief in the gospel is our righteousness, then the gospel does not merely inform us about righteousness but makes us through the Holy Spirit into new, justified persons who already "walk in newness of life" (Rom 6:4). This conviction, common to Catholics and Lutherans, leads into the understanding of church. For if we confess in common that the gospel that gathers the church really is God's creative word, then we must also confess in common that the church itself really is God's creation and as such is a social reality that unites people.

(172) Third, God, who creates the church through his word and has promised that it will abide in the truth and will continue to exist, is faithful to his word and his promise. In the interim, until this promise attains its eschatological goal in the consummation of all things, God effects his faithfulness in the historical form of the church also through structures of historical continuity. Previously, Old Testament Israel was a real historical people which lived from God's promises. To them he gave structures of historical continuity. To be sure, the continuity of the church appears especially to Lutherans to be a constant struggling against the dangers of error and apostasy and finally a victory of God's faithfulness over the constantly recurring unfaithfulness of human beings. This view rests on constitutive ecclesial experiences which are not without their ecclesiological relevance. But Lutherans nonetheless hold that the church will continue in existence and that there are structures which contribute to this continuity, without of course being able to guarantee it.

[232] CA 7; BC 32.

4.5.3   The Areas of Controversy

(173) The questions which arise regarding the relationship between justification and the church may be presented and discussed in four areas: (1) the institutional continuity of the church, (2) the ordained ministry as ecclesial institution, (3) the teaching function of the church's ministry and (4) the jurisdictional function of the church's ministry. Each of these areas relates to the above mentioned reciprocal questioning by Catholics and Lutherans: whether the Lutheran doctrine of justification diminishes the reality of the church; whether the Catholic understanding of the church obscures the gospel as it is explicated by the doctrine of justification.

4.5.3.1   *Institutional Continuity of the Church*

(174) As a creature of the gospel and its proclamation, which is always "external," creative and sustained by God's faithfulness, the church exists continuously through the ages: "one holy Christian church will be and remain forever."[233] Just as everything God creates through his word and sustains in faithfulness to his word has its history, so too the church has its history. It is historical like other creatures, though in a unique way: only the church is promised that it will endure and that the gates of hell will not overcome it.

(175) The historicity of the church is most profoundly bound up with that of the gospel which calls it into being and from which it lives. As the proclaimed and transmitted external word the gospel mediates the abiding faithfulness of God in the midst of the history of this world.

(176) The church created by the gospel is more than the total sum of persons who belong to it here and now. The church is "assembly" not only as congregation which gathers for worship at a particular time and in a particular place. At the same time it is "assembly" in a sense transcending time and place, as church of all people and generations, as the church founded in the Christ-event and existing in

---

[233] CA 7; BC 32.

the preexistent reality of fellowship in the body of Christ. In this sense the church is a communal, social reality of singular character and continuous existence.

(177) If God creates the church as an historical community with a continuous existence by means of the external gospel, this activity of God has its counterpart in the establishment of structural and institutional realities. These serve the continuity of this community, are an expression of it and therefore themselves have a continuous existence. The founding of the church, i.e., its institution in the Christ-event and the establishment of such structural and institutional realities, are therefore indissolubly linked together.

(178) Apostolic preaching, which has its precipitate in the New and the Old Testament canons, together with the sacraments of baptism and the Lord's Supper and the divinely empowered "ministry of reconciliation" (2 Cor 5:18), are such God-appointed means and signs of the continuity of the church, which according to Reformation conviction too, remain constantly in the church. [234] They are institutions in which God makes his creative grace and sustaining faithfulness visible and effective, and which for their part effect and testify to the permanence of the church by their continuity. Their perpetual continuity and that of the church are inseparable.

(179) These realities, which were established along with the foundation of the church, have taken on specific forms in the course of history or have produced other realities which in turn testify to the continuity of the church and serve it, and which therefore likewise have a long-term purpose or have proven themselves to be enduring. This is particularly true regarding the forms which the "ministry of reconciliation" took on very early in the history of the church. But it also holds good for the creeds, dogmas or confessional writings which have arisen in history as an expression of the apostolic faith, and which have their basis in the biblical writings, especially in the confessions of faith found in the New Testament. Our two churches give in part different and indeed

[234] WA 40 I,69; cf. 46,6f.

controversial responses to the question of how far and to what degree these ecclesiastical realities which have arisen in history share in the enduring quality of the realities established when the church was founded. The reasons for the differences are certainly theological and ecclesiological, but very often they also reflect different experiences of the church. But it is not in dispute that (1) these realities arose in the history of the church and were not directly and explicitly established when it was founded, (2) they can certainly give expression to the continuity of the church and be of service to it, and (3) they nevertheless remain capable of renewal and in need of renewal.

(180) Above all, however, it is agreed that all institutional or structural elements of church continuity are and remain instruments of the gospel, which alone creates and sustains the church, not in their own right but only insofar and as long as they testify to the continuity of the church and serve that continuity. Their effectiveness as signs and means of the continuity of the church is limited and called in question when and for as long as their relatedness to and transparency for that gospel are diminished or obscured.

(181) This is true regarding how the church deals with the realities which are integral to its foundation and — according to our common conviction — are indispensable to it, such as the word of God available in the canon of Holy Scripture, the sacraments of baptism and the Lord's Supper and the ministry of reconciliation. But this is especially true of the signs and means of continuity in the church which have emerged in history. Here the idea of the indispensable nature of these signs and instruments of institutional continuity for the church, as advocated not only but especially on the Catholic side, may itself evoke the concern, and indeed reproach that the gospel of the radical gratuitousness of the gift of salvation and unconditional nature of the reception of salvation is being obscured. Consequently, special care is needed to see to it that these instruments and signs of institutional continuity in the church do not cease to function as servants of the gospel, not even when one seems obligated to grant them an ecclesially indispensable and binding character.

4.5.3.2   Ordained Ministry as Institution in the Church

(182) It has already been said in common[235] that the "ministry of reconciliation" which proclaims reconciliation with God "on behalf of Christ" (2 Cor 5:18-20) is one of the indispensable institutional realities given to the church from the beginning to express and serve its continuity.[236] It was also said in common that these realities built into the church, and also their further configurations in history, do not in themselves testify to the church's continuity or bring it about, except in so far as they serve the gospel through which the Holy Spirit creates and sustains the church. The more these institutional realities are thus subordinated to the justification criterion the less we can say that they as such contradict the doctrine of justification and are condemned by it.

(183) This is true also of the ordained ministry in so far as it is by its nature, according to our churches' view, that "ministry of reconciliation" (2 Cor 5:18). The critical assertion that the ordained ministry as an institution of continuity by its very existence runs counter to the doctrine of justification is thus repudiated fundamentally.

(184) However the fact that the Reformation doctrine of justification and its emphasis on the unconditionality of the gift of salvation has at times been understood as questioning the necessity of the ordained ministry and the legitimacy of its institutional, ecclesial form calls for an even more pointed rejoinder.

(185) First of all it must be stressed, as the previous Roman Catholic-Lutheran dialogue has done, that the Lutheran Reformation knows no such ecclesiological consequence of the doctrine of justification. There is no contradiction between the doctrine of justification and the idea of an ordained ministry instituted by God and necessary for the church. Quite the opposite. The Augsburg Confession already makes this clear, with its characteristic transition from the article on

---

[235] See above 178.
[236] Cf. *The Ministry in the Church*, 17.

justification[237] to that on the church's ministry.[238] There justifying faith is grounded in the gospel which the ordained ministry is to proclaim in word and sacraments. Article 14 of the Augsburg Confession excludes the idea, which only arose in the nineteenth century, that "the church's ministry" or the "preaching ministry" could mean anything other than the ecclesiastical institution of the ordained ministry. For Luther and the Lutheran Confessions, the church's ministry and the gospel are so closely united that they can both be spoken of in identical terms[239] and can let the church be founded on the ministry.[240] In a similar sense Lutheran orthodoxy taught that the triune God is "the primary efficient cause" of the church and that the church's ministry is the "efficient cause which God uses to gather his church."[241]

(186) In agreement with the Reformation, and without contradicting the Reformation doctrine of justification, we can therefore repeat what has already been said in the Lutheran-Roman Catholic dialogue on the ministry: "... the existence of a special ministry is abidingly constitutive for the church."[242]

(187) These points show that Reformation thought provides no basis for fearing that the very existence of an ordained ministry as necessary institution for the church obscures the gospel. Above all it must be seen how the institution of the ministry is positively in line with the gospel and its explication through the doctrine of justification.

(188) If the New Testament — and with it the Lutheran Reformation — sees the special character of the ordained ministry in the fact that ministers are called to preach reconciliation publicly "on behalf of Christ" (2 Cor 5:20),[243] and thus stand "over against the community"

---

[237] CA 4; BC 30.
[238] CA 5; BC 31.
[239] Apol 7,20; BC 171; WA 30 III, 88.
[240] *Tractatus,* 25.
[241] Johann Gerhard, *Loci theologici*, XXII,V,37,40.
[242] *The Ministry in the Church*, 18.
[243] Cf. Apol 7,28; BC 173.

even while "within the community,"[244] this corresponds directly to the inmost concern of the doctrine of justification itself. At stake is that God in Christ approaches human beings "from outside" for their salvation notwithstanding everything they know, are capable of and are. Human beings — even believers — cannot say to themselves what God has to say to them and cannot bring themselves to that salvation which God alone has prepared for them. This structural movement "outside us and for us"[245] is constitutive of the saving revelation of God in Christ. It is continued in the proclamation of the gospel and must continue there if the gospel is not to be obscured. For this, God establishes the ordained ministry, and consequently, from among his many followers, Jesus calls his emissaries, in whom his mission from the Father is continued (cf. Jn 20:21; 17:18), and of whom it is true to say "whoever listens to you listens to me" (Lk 10:16) and "whoever welcomes you welcomes me, and whoever welcomes me welcomes the one who sent me" (Mt 10:40).

(189) Thus not only does the institution of the ordained ministry not contradict the gospel as it is explicated by the doctrine of justification, but corresponds to it and in the last analysis receives its character of indispensability for the church from that correspondence. The Lutheran-Roman Catholic dialogue on the church's ministry had drawn attention to this also when it stated with the Accra document of that time and with the later BEM statement[246] that "the presence of this ministry in the community 'signifies the priority of divine initiative and authority in the Church's existence'."[247]

(190) It is no contradiction of the close connection between the ministry and the gospel but is rather in line with it, that for the ministry and for ordained ministers the doctrine of justification as explication of the gospel must be the criterion for their own self-understanding and actions. For although the connection between the ministry and the gospel certainly exists, it is no guarantee against abuse and false doctrine. Just as the New Testament knows of and

---

[244] *The Ministry in the Church*, 23.

[245] *extra nos pro nobis.*

[246] Cf. *Baptism, Eucharist and Ministry*, Ministry, 8, 12, 42.

[247] *The Ministry in the Church*, 20.

warns against "false teachers"[248] and "false apostles"[249] (2 Pet 2:1; 2 Cor 11:13), it is also part of the historical experience of the church that the office, in its bearers and their ministry, may come to contradict the gospel (cf. Gal. 1:6ff; 2:14). The way this experience registers in the ecclesiology and church law of our two churches differs in part. The possibility of a conflict between the ministry and the gospel and thus the need for the church to stand guard over the primacy of the gospel are however seen and affirmed on both sides.

(191) The conviction that the doctrine of justification must, as an explication of the gospel, be the critical yardstick for our understanding and exercise of the ministry is applied in the Lutheran Reformation and the Lutheran churches in a special and for them significant way. It relates to the specific forms which the divinely instituted ministry has assumed in the course of history. This is true above all in regard to the specific formation of the ecclesial ministry of leadership (*episkopé*). The development of the ministry into an episcopate standing in a historic succession, i.e., the continuity of apostolic succession which occurred already very early in history[250] was fully affirmed by the Lutheran Reformation and emphatically championed[251] just as other church realities were affirmed and conserved which had come into being in the course of history (e.g. the biblical canon, the creeds of the ancient church). For Lutheran thinking too it is entirely possible to acknowledge that the historical development of an episcopate in a historic succession was not something purely within the sphere of history, set in motion only by sociological and political factors, but that it "has taken place with the help of the Holy Spirit" and that it "constitutes something essential for the church."[252]

(192) However, Lutherans cannot agree when something is seen in this historically developed formation of the ministry whose existence plays a part in determining the very being of the church. The reason is not simply the ecclesial experience of the Reformation,

---

[248] *pseudodidaskaloi.*
[249] *pseudoapostoloi.*
[250] Cf. *The Ministry in the Church*, 40-49; 59-66.
[251] Cf. Apol 14; BC 214f.
[252] *The Ministry in the Church*, 49; cf. 50.

namely that, at least in central Europe, the Reformation struggled for the truth of the gospel not only without the support of the church's episcopate, but even against its resistance. The deeper reason is the concern that putting episcopacy on such a level endangers the unconditional nature of the gift of salvation and its reception. And that is precisely what is at stake in the Reformation doctrine of justification. For this unconditionality necessarily implies that only that may be considered necessary for the church to be church which is already given by Jesus Christ himself as means of salvation. If ecclesial structures, which emerged in history, are elevated to that level, they become pre-conditions for receiving salvation and so, in the Lutheran view, are put illegitimately on the same level with the gospel proclaimed in word and sacrament which alone is necessary for salvation and the church.

(193) Here a clear difference between Catholics and Lutherans reveals itself in the theological and ecclesiological evaluation of the episcopal office in historic succession, a difference which has been repeatedly noted in the Catholic-Lutheran dialogue up to now. [253]

(194) According to Roman Catholic understanding there is an historic development of the then permanent form of the ordained ministry. This is especially true of its post-apostolic organization into "bishops, priests and other ministers." [254] Here of course we have to consider that this post-apostolic organization and identification of distinctions in the ministry is already attested to incipiently in the Bible and was introduced in the transition from the "emerging" to the "developed" church.

(195) The shared Catholic-Lutheran conviction that the historical emergence of the ministry's structure is not simply to be traced back to human — sociological and political — factors but "has taken place with the help of the Holy Spirit" [255] is, in the Catholic view, understood and prioritized differently than in Lutheran thought. Unlike the Lutherans, Catholics see a "divine institution" in the organization of

---

[253] *The Ministry in the Church*, 46f; especially *Facing Unity*, 94-98.
[254] DS 1776.
[255] *The Ministry in the Church*, 49.

the ministry as it has developed through history, i.e., a development led, willed and testified to by divine providence. [256] Under the operation of the Holy Spirit within the apostolic tradition, episcopacy and apostolic succession as orderly transmission of the ordained ministry have developed as the expression, means and criterion of the continuity of the tradition in post-apostolic times. Thus in the providence of God the bishops "by divine institution" [257] are successors to the apostles. The task of the apostles to tend the church of God continues in the episcopacy and bishops are to exercise it continually.

(196) The episcopate and apostolic succession as the orderly transmission of the ordained ministry in the church are therefore in the Catholic view essential for the church as church, and so are necessary and indispensable. Nevertheless word and sacrament are the two pillars of the church which are necessary for salvation. The episcopate and apostolic succession stand in service as ministry to what is necessary for salvation, so that the word will be authentically preached and the sacraments rightly celebrated. The episcopate and apostolic succession serve to safeguard the apostolic tradition, the content of which is expressed in the rule of faith. The Spirit of God uses the episcopate in order to identify the church in every historical situation with its apostolic origin, to integrate the faithful in the one universal faith of the church and just so through the episcopate to make its liberating force effective. In this sense the episcopate is in the Catholic view a necessary service of the gospel which is itself necessary for salvation.

(197) The difference between the Catholic and Lutheran views on the theological and ecclesiological evaluation of the episcopate is thus not so radical that a Lutheran rejection or even indifference toward this ministry stands in opposition to the Catholic assertion of its ecclesial indispensability. The question is rather one of a clear gradation in the evaluation of this ministry, which can be and has been described on the Catholic side by predicates such as "necessary" or

---

[256] Cf. DS 1776: *"hierarchiam divina ordinatione institutam;"* cf. LG 28: "Thus the divinely established ecclesiastical ministry is exercised on different levels by those who from antiquity have been called bishops, priests, and deacons."
[257] LG 20.

"indispensable" and on the Lutheran side as "important," "meaning-ful," and thus "desirable."[258]

(198) For a proper understanding of this Catholic-Lutheran difference in the evaluation of the episcopate, it is necessary to observe that behind it lie two different correlations of salvation and church.

(199) According to the Lutheran doctrine of justification and the Lutheran understanding of the church, it is only through the proclamation of the gospel in word and sacraments, which ordained ministers are called to do, that the Holy Spirit effects justifying faith[259] and that the church is created and preserved.[260] The church exists in the full sense of the word where this saving gospel proclamation takes place.[261]

(200) Following this ecclesiological line, nothing good and "profitable"[262] for ecclesial communion which exists alongside the gospel proclaimed in word and sacraments may be considered ecclesially necessary, in the strict sense of that word, lest the one thing necessary for salvation — the gospel — be endangered.[263]

(201) According to the Catholic understanding of faith there is also a stable correlation of church and salvation which cannot be dissolved. Therefore Vatican II calls the church "the universal sacrament of salvation."[264] It is sign and instrument of salvation for all humanity so that without the church there is no salvation. Within this context, however, Catholic thinking further differentiates the subjective and personal consideration of human salvation by reason of God's

---

[258] Cf. Apol 14; BC 214f; WA 26,195f; *The Ministry in the Church*, 65f, 49 and 50; *Facing Unity*, 106, 97.

[259] Cf. CA 5; BC 31.

[260] Cf. CA 7; BC 32; WA 7,721; see above 36.

[261] See above 85.

[262] Apol 7,34; BC 175.

[263] Apol 7,30-37 interprets CA 7: The question in the *nec necesse est* is not whether what is added in the church to proclaim the gospel is "profitable" and "necessary" for the church. The main question is rather whether it is "necessary for righteousness" (*necessarius ad iustitiam*). BC 173ff.

[264] LG 48.

grace and the objective and ecclesiological view of the church as recipient and mediator of salvation. Therefore the Second Vatican Council maintains with regard to non-Catholic Christians that "many elements of sanctification and of truth can be found outside of her visible structure" [265] and that the non-Catholic churches and communities are used by Christ's Spirit as "means of salvation." [266] In addition Vatican II says in relation to non-Christians that God's saving activity is at once visibly and invisibly at work among those who have not yet received the gospel and that God "can lead those inculpably ignorant of the gospel to that faith without which it is impossible to please Him." [267] To this extent there is, according to Catholic understanding, a correlation between salvation and church consisting not only in the church membership of those who hear the word in faith and receive the sacraments fruitfully, but there is also an ordination to the church on the basis of the visible and hidden saving work of God's grace outside the church which can lead to saving faith.

(202) This differentiation is also expressed regarding the ecclesial necessity of the episcopal office in apostolic succession, something which is not necessary for the salvation of individual persons. Because of such a differentiation it is possible for Catholics to assert the necessity of this office without thereby contradicting the doctrine of justification. Thus the episcopal office is understood in the church as a necessary ministry of the gospel which itself is necessary for salvation.

(203) Even so, Catholics will have to take seriously and answer the Lutheran question. If Catholics hold that the Lord's Supper celebrated in Lutheran churches has "because of the lack [defectus] of the sacrament of orders ... not preserved the genuine and total reality [substantia] of the Eucharistic mystery," [268] does that not, after all, show that they regard the episcopal office in historic succession as the regular transmitter of the ordained ministry in the church, and so

[265] LG 8; cf. UR 3.
[266] UR 3.
[267] AG 7.
[268] UR 22.

indirectly as necessary for salvation? Catholics must answer that an ecclesiology focused on the concept of succession, as held in the Catholic Church, need in no way deny the saving presence of the Lord in a eucharist celebrated by Lutherans.

(204) The difference in the theological and ecclesiological evaluation of the episcopal office in historic succession loses its sharpness when Lutherans attribute such a value to the episcopate that regaining full communion in this office seems important and desirable, and when Catholics recognize that "the ministry in the Lutheran churches exercises essential functions of the ministry that Jesus Christ instituted in his church"[269] and does not contest the point that the Lutheran churches are church.[270] The difference in evaluating the historic episcopate is thereby interpreted in such a way that the doctrine of justification is no longer at stake and consequently it is also possible to advocate theologically the regaining of full communion in the episcopate.[271]

4.5.3.3 Binding Church Doctrine and the Teaching Function of the Ministry

(205) The church's abiding in the truth, which is God's promise and also his commission to the church, requires inescapably that the church must distinguish the truth of the gospel from error. That means, however, the church must teach. This does not at all contradict the Reformation doctrine of justification because its own claim is to promote this very distinction between truth and error in a fundamental way.

(206) The commission to continue in the truth, like the promise to bring this about, holds good for the church as a whole. Our churches are agreed on this. We also agree that it is primarily the Spirit of God, promised to the church and dwelling in it[272] who enables it so to continue and gives it the authority to distinguish truth and error in a

---

[269] The Ministry in the Church, 77.
[270] Cf. UR 19-23.
[271] Cf. Facing Unity, 117-139.
[272] See above 3.2.3.

binding way, that is, to teach. [273] Finally, we agree that for his activity God in the Holy Spirit makes use of temporal instruments and circumstances which he himself has bestowed upon the church as a temporal and creaturely entity; [274] and that the ministry is one of these instruments and circumstances. [275] There is no tension between this and the doctrine of justification as criterion for the church's life and activity.

(207) It is in fact true of the Lutheran as much as of the Roman Catholic Church that like the church in every age it is a teaching church which sees itself under the continuing commission to preserve the truth of the gospel and to reject error. Its catechisms, especially Luther's Large Catechism, and most particularly the Confessions with their "teaching" and "rejecting" exemplify this. [276]

(208) The difference between our churches only begins to surface where the issue is how the church's responsibility for teaching is exercised. When the Roman Catholic Church attributes a special responsibility and authority for teaching to the ministry and in particular to the episcopate, this in itself still does not imply any essential difference from the Lutheran view and practice. For in the Lutheran view too the ministry, along with its mission and authority to preach the gospel and inseparably from them, is given a responsibility for the "purity" of the proclaimed gospel and the "right" administration of the sacraments "according to the Gospel." [277] It was also axiomatic for the Reformation that there are ordered ministries in the church such as the teaching office of theologians and faculties who had the right and duty to distinguish truth and error in a special way. Luther was himself able to assert his rights as a theological teacher in face of the ecclesiastical authorities who had themselves appointed him as such.

[273] Cf. Malta Report, 18.
[274] See above 4.5.2.
[275] See above 4.5.3.1.
[276] CA 1: *"Ecclesiae magno consensu apud nos docent ..."* "Our churches teach with great unanimity ..."(BC 27); cf. CA 1-21 (BC 27ff), and the conclusion in the first part of the Confessio Augustana which says: "This is just about a summary of the doctrines that are preached and taught in our churches" (BC 47).
[277] CA 7; BC 32.

(209) Following the medieval tradition, it was extremely common for the theological faculties in areas of the Lutheran Reformation to exercise something like an ecclesial teaching function. Nor was it contested on the Reformation side that a special responsibility for teaching belongs to the bishops: they are entitled "according to divine right ... to ... judge doctrine and condemn doctrine that is contrary to the gospel" and congregations are therefore in duty "bound to be obedient to the bishops according to the saying of Christ in Luke 10:16, 'He who hears you hears me'."[278] The episcopal structure was however not preserved in most churches of the Reformation.[279] Very early in the German lands (about 1527) there developed within the framework of ecclesial governance by princes an alternative system for supra-parish doctrinal oversight by creating superintendents, visitors or visitation commissions. They exercised the function of a teaching office by seeing to it that parish preaching and the administration of the sacraments were true to the gospel. "Also in our day there is interpretation and development of church doctrine in Lutheran churches through the decisions of the appropriate ecclesial authorities" (bishops synods, church councils) in which office-bearers, church members and theological teachers together play a part.[280] Nevertheless significant differences appear here too.

(210) The Reformers thought that the promise and responsibility which held good for the whole church was concentrated to such an extent in the teaching ministry exercised by bishops and the Pope in the Roman church that the inerrancy promised to the church as a whole had shifted to the bishops and the Pope. This, so it was said, revealed the new Roman "definition of the church," which was rejected.[281] Regarding the promise and commission to abide in the truth the following principle held good for the Reformation: "Nor should that be transferred to the popes which is the prerogative of the true church: that they are pillars of the truth and that they do not err."[282]

278 CA 28,21f; BC 84.
279 Cf. *The Ministry in the Church*, 42.
280 Cf. ibid. 55.
281 Apol 7,23-27, especially 23; BC 172f.
282 Apol 7,27; BC 173.

(211) Here, according to Reformation conviction, the critical function of the doctrine of justification comes into play. In this, the primary question is not that the church as the congregation of the faithful (*congregatio fidelium*) might take second place to the church as "supreme outward monarchy;"[283] or that the equality of the people of God might be canceled out. And it certainly is not a question of a modern ideal of freedom or the application to the church of the idea of the sovereignty of the people. The issue is, first and foremost, the primacy of the gospel over the church — the freedom, sovereignty and ultimate binding nature of the gospel as God's word of grace.

(212) The Reformation conviction is that this gospel, even if proclaimed in the church, and by ministers called to serve "in Christ's place and stead"[284] cannot without reservations and with no questions asked be consigned to an ecclesiastical ministry to preserve. For in so far as this ministry, like every church institution, is carried out by human beings who are capable of error, not only would the danger of error be increased thereby, because the error would then take on binding force in the church, but also and above all a sovereignty and ultimate binding force would attach to the decisions and stipulations of this ministry and its representatives which are reserved for the gospel alone. That is why what people teach in the church must ultimately be measured against the gospel alone. Only then is it certain that the church relies on God's word and not human words.

(213) For the sake of the gospel, the Reformation doctrine of justification therefore requires that the church's ministry and its decisions should as a matter of principle be open to examination by the whole people of God. As a matter of principle justification debars them from insulating themselves from such an examination. In regard to its decisions the teaching ministry must permit "question or censure,"[285] as the Apology says, by the church as a whole, for which the promise of abiding in the truth holds good, and which is the people of God, the body of Christ and the temple of the Holy Spirit.

[283] Apol 7:23; BC 172.
[284] Apol 7,28; BC 173.
[285] Apol 7,23; BC 172.

Otherwise it seems doubtful from a Reformation perspective that the teaching ministry serves the word of God and is not above it. [286]

(214) The binding nature of church teaching is not canceled out by this, but is made subject to a reservation. In the Reformation view the teaching of the church or of a teaching ministry must take place precisely in this dialectical tension between the claim of its binding nature and the reservation relating to that binding nature. This will demonstrate that the teaching ministry respects the independence of the gospel and its ultimate binding nature, which is nothing other than the independence and binding nature of the grace of God. In this church teaching as such demonstrates its own conformity with the gospel.

(215) It is thus clear that the doctrine of justification certainly does not lead Reformation thinking into a depreciation, far less a rejection, of binding church teaching and of a teaching ministry of the church. The churches of the Lutheran Reformation themselves carry out binding teaching and themselves have organs or ministries for the church's teaching. They even have displayed the willingness, and indeed the "deep desire" [287] to recognize for themselves the church's teaching ministry in its traditional form. [288] What they insist on is solely that this teaching and this teaching ministry be in accordance with the gospel in their self-understanding and exercise, and do not contradict the gospel. [289]

(216) The problem of a tension between the claim to and the reservation related to binding teaching arises for Catholics too. Admittedly from their point of view the matter has a different weight and value. According to Catholic teaching the church as a whole is "the pillar and bulwark of the truth" (1 Tim 3:15). "The body of the faithful as a whole ... cannot err in matters of belief" as it receives the "supernatural sense of the faith" from the Spirit of truth. [290] Within the

---

[286] Cf. DV 10.
[287] Apol 14,1 and 2; BC 214.
[288] Cf. Malta Report, 66; *The Ministry in the Church*, 65f, 73, 80; *Facing Unity*, 97.
[289] Cf. Malta Report, 66.
[290] LG 12.

people of God the bishops in communion with the bishop of Rome are the authentic teachers of the faith by virtue of their episcopal ordination as successors in the presiding ministry of a local church. [291] But their teaching office remains anchored in the life of faith of the whole people of God, who share in the discovery of and in witnessing to the truth. Thus "the vigilance with regard to the apostolicity of the faith that belongs to the bishop's duty, is bound up with the responsibility for the faith borne by the whole Christian people," [292] and thus bishops exercise their teaching ministry "only in community with the whole church" and "in a many-sided exchange regarding faith with believers, priests, and theologians," [293] for the whole "People of God shares also in Christ's prophetic office." [294]

(217) "While it is possible for the individual bishop to fall away from the continuity of the apostolic faith ... Catholic tradition holds that the episcopate as a whole is nevertheless kept firm in the truth of the gospel." [295] The bishops have to watch over the continuity of the apostolic faith, while being bound to the canon of Scripture and the apostolic tradition: the "teaching office is not above the word of God but serves it, teaching only what has been handed on." [296] It has the task of listening reverently to the word of God, preserving it in holiness and expounding it faithfully. [297] The same is valid for the priest. "The task of priests is not to teach their own wisdom but God's Word." [298] This submission to the canon of the Scriptures and the apostolic tradition is the basic criterion for the response of faith, especially in borderline cases, so that according to Augustine and Thomas Aquinas it can be said: "One must deny one's consent even to bishops when it happens that they err and speak in a manner that contradicts the canonical texts." [299]

---

[291] Cf. LG 25.
[292] *Facing Unity*, 110.
[293] *The Ministry in the Church*, 51.
[294] LG 12
[295] *The Ministry in the Church*, 62; cf. LG 25.
[296] DV 10; cf. *The Ministry in the Church*, 50.
[297] Cf. ibid; *The Ministry in the Church*, 5O and 62.
[298] PO 4.
[299] *Facing Unity*, 110 and footnote 157.

(218) The church can make infallible decisions on doctrine, as happened in the early church at ecumenical councils. [300] These decisions explicate the revelation that has taken place once for all, and are made in harmony with the faith of the entire people of God, certainly not against them. [301] These decisions, when made under specific conditions, are valid of themselves and do not need any subsequent formal approval, though they of course "depend on extensive reception in order to have living power and spiritual fruitfulness in the church." [302]

(219) Decisions of the church's teaching ministry are indeed binding — as dogma, even definitively binding. But the church knows it is the pilgrim people of God on the march. Hence recognition of the truth in theology and dogma is fragmentary and often onesided, since it is frequently a response to errors that have taken an extreme position. Dogma is historically conditioned and therefore open to corrections, deeper understanding and "new expressions." [303] The church nevertheless believes that the Holy Spirit guides it into the truth and preserves it from error when solemn definitions are made. When the teaching ministry appeals to the Holy Spirit (cf. Acts 15:28), this does not run counter to the criterion of the doctrine of justification. For the question here is not about conditions for salvation, but the criteria of our knowledge of revelation. The message of the radical gratuity of the gift of salvation, and of the unconditionality of the reception of salvation, is not obscured by the institution of councils, because their role is to witness to the truth of revelation and to protect this truth against erroneous opinions.

(220) The Catholic understanding of faith holds that the gospel is interpreted by the consensus of a council and this can therefore in special cases bring forth a definitively binding statement (a dogma in the Catholic view) on which members of the church can rely as an expression of the gospel. Even if faith does not rest in the formulation

[300] Cf. among others DS 265.
[301] DS 3073f.
[302] *The Ministry in the Church*, 52.
[303] Cf. *Mysterium ecclesiae*, 5, Statement by the Vatican Congregation for the Doctrine of the Faith.

but in the reality, that is, in the truth of the gospel, it nevertheless needs the formulation in which the gospel is expressed, the wording of which must be very carefully heeded in a critical situation (cf. 1 Cor 15:2; 4:6).

(221) On the other hand, also in Catholic understanding, a dogmatic statement is not simply a given about which no further questions may be asked. "The tradition which comes from the apostles develops in the Church with the help of the Holy Spirit. For there is a growth in the understanding of the realities and the words which have been handed down. This happens through the contemplation and study made by believers, who treasure these things in their hearts ..., through the intimate understanding of spiritual things they experience, and through the preaching of those who have received through episcopal succession the sure gift of truth. For, as the centuries succeed one another, the Church constantly moves forward toward the fullness of divine truth until the words of God reach their complete fulfillment in her."[304] Looked at in this light, the transmission of faith, official doctrinal proclamation and the history of dogma are complex hermeneutical processes in which all the faithful, members of the teaching office and theologians, are participants even if in differing ways.[305] Abiding in the truth of the gospel does not exclude the painstaking quest for the truth. It is not carried out alone by one component of the church but is due in the last analysis to the support and guidance of God's Spirit who exercises control through the fellowship of the whole people of God.

(222) This comparison of the Lutheran and Catholic understanding of binding doctrines shows, despite all the different emphases and a fair number of critical questions, that binding teaching need not contradict justification. Catholics and Lutherans agree that binding teaching illuminates the truth of the gospel, on which truth alone members of the church may and should rely in living and dying and which alone sustains their faith. They agree that, for example, in the councils that confess the faith in the Trinity and in Jesus Christ the truth of the gospel is explicated. There are considerable differences,

[304] DV 8.
[305] Cf. DV 10.

to be sure, as to how the truth of the gospel is affirmed. Even if Catholics cannot in the same way appropriate the Lutheran dialectic in which the claim to a binding character for doctrine contrasts with a reservation as to that binding character, and if they ask whether there is not a danger here that the opinion of individuals will be identified with the truth of the gospel, they too are aware of the provisional nature of human knowledge of the truth, even in the ultimately binding decisions of the teaching office. If Lutherans pose the above mentioned question concerning the Catholic form of binding teaching, they are nevertheless faced with the task of rethinking "the problem of the teaching office and the teaching authority" and of reflecting especially on the council as an institution, that is, as "the locus for the expression of the consensus of all Christendom,"[306] and of its importance to which the Reformation always firmly held.[307]

4.5.3.4 *Church Jurisdiction and the Jurisdictional Function of the Ministry*

(223) The questions of doctrine and the church's teaching office, and of ecclesial jurisdiction and the jurisdictional function of the ministry are very close to each other and show clear parallels. In part the two questions even overlap, in so far as decisions of the church's teaching ministry are juridically binding.

(224) Catholics and Lutherans together say that God, who establishes institutional entities in his grace and faithfulness, and who uses them to preserve the church in the truth of the gospel, also uses church law and legal ordinances for this purpose.

(225) Thus Lutherans cannot say that gospel and church on one side and ecclesiastical law on the other are mutually exclusive or that the doctrine of justification prohibits the development of binding ecclesial law. The very fact that in Reformation lands legally binding church orders (*Kirchenordnungen*) came into being at a very early date, and that in their doctrinal sections (*corpora doctrinae*), which

---

[306] *The Ministry in the Church*, 56 and 73.
[307] See above 211-214.

were replaced later by the confessions, the doctrine of justification has a central place, shows that justification itself participated in the juridically binding nature of these church orders. Constitutions of today's Lutheran churches indicate this also.

(226) When, however, it comes to the understanding of church law and its binding nature; when the question is raised to what extent and in what sense the church, and especially the ordained ministry, have the authority to make legally binding decisions and regulations; and when it is asked to what extent such decisions, once taken, can be critically examined on the basis of the gospel — then a difference between Catholics and Lutherans becomes evident, just as it does with the question of doctrine and the teaching ministry.

(227) This difference, however, is to be seen in the context of common basic convictions which have already been highlighted in the Lutheran-Roman Catholic dialogue.

— In regard to church law as a whole the principle holds good for both churches that "the salvation of souls ... must always be the supreme law."[308]
— That in turn means that according to common conviction all church law and all development of ecclesial law are related and subordinated to the service of the gospel. "The church is permanently bound in its ordering to the gospel which is irrevocably prior to it;" the gospel is "the criterion for a concrete church order."[309]
— Even where, in line with the traditional view and terminology, the character of "divine law," a *ius divinum*, is attributed to church legislation, it has a historical shape and form, and it is therefore both possible and necessary to renew and reshape it.[310]

(228) These common basic convictions show that church law, notwithstanding its claim to be binding, is by its nature and by

[308] CIC, Can. 1752: "*salus animarum semper suprema lex;*" The Code of Canon Law, 1983, London, 310; Malta Report, 32: For church law, "the final decisive viewpoint must be that of the salvation of the individual believer."
[309] Malta Report, 33.
[310] Cf. *ibid*. 31 and 33.

definition subject to a reservation as to its binding nature. This is of crucial importance, because it is precisely the critical demand raised by the doctrine of justification regarding all church legislation and so also to all church legal authorities. No church legislation can claim to be binding in such a manner that it is necessary for salvation, thus equalling the ultimate binding nature of the gospel which is itself the binding nature of grace. In so far as this demand is not met, church law becomes subject to criticism from the doctrine of justification. On this our churches agree in principle. It is important that this agreement should also be maintained in church practice; but whether, how and to what extent this happens in our churches must be verified from one case to another.

(229) These basic convictions apply also to the question to what extent and in what way a jurisdictional function is appropriate to the ordained ministry. The Reformation too can in fact attribute a jurisdictional function to the ministry but in so doing it emphasizes the primacy of the gospel and, essentially, those limitations which are recognized in common by Catholics and Lutherans. [311]

(230) This is the overall intention of Article 28 of the Augsburg Confession. [312] It develops a view of the power *(potestas)* of the bishops, which unequivocally includes jurisdictional functions. At the same time it seeks to guarantee the harmony of this ministry and its exercise with the gospel, doing this essentially in the framework of the basic convictions outlined above.

(231) The proper tasks of the bishop, which appertain basically to the pastor also — because of a theological lack of clarity in the differentiation between bishop and pastor — are, according to CA 28, "to preach the Gospel," "to forgive ... sins," "to administer ... the sacraments," to "condemn doctrine that is contrary to the Gospel" and to "exclude from the Christian community." [313] They can be summed

[311] See above 227.
[312] CA 28: The Power of Bishops; BC 81ff.
[313] CA 28,5 and 21; BC 81 and 84.

up in the terms "power of keys,"[314] "the office of preaching"[315] or "jurisdiction."[316] These show that according to the Reformation view the ministry as a pastoral office includes jurisdictional functions, certainly in such a way that these functions do not become autonomous but remain bound up in the total pastoral responsibility of the ministry and so preserve their pastoral character.

(232) Over against these functions of the ordained ministry which are "necessary for salvation"[317] and are in this sense by "divine right"[318] but which must be exercised "not by human power but by God's word alone,"[319] the duty of the congregation to obey holds good.[320] It is an obligation, however, which is paired with the duty to refuse obedience should the ministry violate the gospel in its exercise of these functions.[321]

(233) Alongside this the bishops can undoubtedly exercise yet another kind of jurisdiction[322] from marriage legislation through ceremonial laws and regulations for worship to decrees for fasts and so on. Such regulations in the last analysis serve the orderly common life of the congregation[323] and they may be changed, replaced and even abrogated.[324] Here too indeed a duty on the part of the congregation to obey holds good[325] but it is fundamentally different in kind. It does not end only where these regulations of the ministry which relate to church law violate the gospel in their content. It already ends where they are imposed as "necessary for salvation"[326] and binding on the conscience,[327] and here changes into a duty to refuse obedience. For

---

[314] CA 28,5 and 8; BC 81.
[315] CA 28,10; BC 82.
[316] CA 28,20f. and 29; BC 84f.
[317] CA 28,8f; BC 82.
[318] CA 28,21; BC 84.
[319] Ibid.
[320] CA 28,22; ibid.
[321] CA 28,23ff; ibid.
[322] CA 28,29ff; BC 85f.
[323] CA 28,53 and 55; BC 89f.
[324] CA 28,66f and 73f; BC 92ff.
[325] CA 28,55; BC 90.
[326] CA 28,43-48; 50; 53 and frequently; BC 88ff.
[327] CA 28,42; 49; 53; 64; 77 and frequently; ibid.

these regulations are already contradicting the "teaching concerning faith," that is, of the "righteousness of faith"[328] and "Christian liberty," i.e., the freedom of the Christian from the law,[329] and they thereby become subject to criticism by the doctrine of justification.

(234) It is a Lutheran conviction that there is a legitimate jurisdictional function of the ordained ministry in this context which is defined by the doctrine of justification.

(235) According to the Catholic view the above mentioned common basic convictions also mark the jurisdictional authority of the episcopate.[330] The exercise of law and canonical practice is always to be seen in its pastoral intention and within a concern for the salvation of humanity.

(236) The authority and power of bishops is part of their being shepherds and presiders over the church. It is founded in the divine mission that Christ entrusted to the apostles,[331] to hand on the gospel which "is for all time the source of all life for the Church."[332] This power also includes the right and the duty to regulate everything in the church which pertains to the ordering of worship and of the apostolate. But it should be carried out in accordance with the example of the Good Shepherd Jesus Christ.[333] Bishops exercise their pastoral and jurisdictional authority in the name of Christ and personally, i.e., as their special, regular and direct power, in communion with the Bishop of Rome.[334] In this connection they have always to take into account the fact that every ordering of the church develops from a permanently given basis, namely, that the church is a community of faith and sacraments. The proclamation of the word of God and the celebration of the sacraments constitute the church and determine its nature, because the Lord of the church effects salvation in them. The

---

[328] CA 28,37; 50; 52; 66 and frequently; BC 86ff.
[329] CA 28,51; 60; 64 and frequently; BC 89ff.
[330] See above 227.
[331] LG 27.
[332] LG 20.
[333] LG 27.
[334] LG 27; CD 3.

binding force of a church law therefore presupposes the conviction that the church is a faith and sacramental community. The aim of the law and canons of the church is to serve the church's order and to express its unity while contributing to the good order of the care of souls. Thus church order, with law and canons, arises out of the nature of the church as a faith and sacramental community.

(237) Catholic teaching insists that no one may be coerced into believing nor be "forced to act in a manner contrary to his own beliefs" in religious matters. [335] Even the call of God to serve him in spirit and in truth, though it binds human beings in their conscience to obey that call, does not coerce them into doing so. [336] And while church norms and laws can indeed be binding in conscience on Christians as members of the church, they cannot "release a member of the church from his direct responsibility to God." [337]

(238) The Catholic-Lutheran dialogue has stressed that "the church is permanently bound in its ordering to the gospel which is irrevocably prior to it ... The gospel, however, can be the criterion for a concrete church order only in living relationship with contemporary social realities. Just as there is a legitimate explication of the gospel in dogmas and confessions, so there also exists a historical actualization of law in the church." [338] In this sense the *Codex Iuris Canonici* of 1983 also attempts a reordering of Catholic church legislation in the light of Vatican II, in order to correspond better with the church's mission of salvation. In particular the ecclesiological guidelines of the Dogmatic Constitution, *Lumen Gentium,* and the Pastoral Constitution, *Gaudium et Spes,* constitute the hermeneutical framework for this. "Over the course of time, the Catholic Church has been wont to revise and renew the laws of its sacred discipline so that, maintaining always fidelity to the Divine Founder, these laws may be truly in accord with the salvific mission entrusted to the Church ... This new

---

[335] DH 2 *(in re religiosa neque aliquis cogatur ad agendum contra suam conscientiam);* 12.
[336] DH 11.
[337] Malta Report, 32, referring to DH 2; 10-12.
[338] Malta Report, 33.

Code can be viewed as a great effort to translate the conciliar ecclesiological teaching into canonical terms." [339]

(239) Catholic theology draws attention to the fact that it is God's saving activity, not ecclesiastical lawgivers with their legislation, which establishes the fellowship of believers and therefore brings people into a new social situation with obligations: that of the believers' fellowship with each other and with God. This new social situation is expressed by the ecclesiastical lawgiver in legal ordinances. The point of ecclesiastical legislation is to help believers perceive and fulfill their rights and duties as well as possible in the light of the faith, and thus to contribute to the realization of the saving mission of the church.

(240) Because church legislation can be seen as a normative function of the tradition of faith, and because the binding force of church laws is ultimately founded in the binding force of faith, church law differs from every other law. Because of the binding force of faith, the church legislator addresses the religious conscience, and thus ecclesiastically binding norms presuppose a free decision of faith. Consequently it is possible for a discrepancy, and thus a case of conflict, to arise between the obligation of a church law and the conscience of the individual Christian believer. Catholic theology, of course, does not generally speak of a "reservation" regarding the binding character of church laws, but in individual cases it does take into account the possibility of conflict. The salvation of human beings counts as supreme law. If in a concrete instance the application of the existing canons may prejudice or even endanger a person's salvation, that constitutes a case in which Christian believers who are quite willing to obey church law and have also shown this in practical living may, and even must, nevertheless come to a decision which is against the letter of the law, because on the basis of faith they see themselves entitled or even obliged to make that decision as a matter of conscience.

[339] John Paul II, Apostolic Constitution, *Sacrae Disciplinae Leges*, promulgating the new Code of 1983; *The Code of Canon Law,* 1983, London, XIff.

(241) Despite different ecclesiological starting points and a different frame of reference, fundamental common elements and correspondences do exist between Lutherans and Catholics on the matter of the doctrines of justification and salvation and their relation to the jurisdictional authority of the ordained ministry. The task of church laws is to serve the salvation of the individual.

* * *

(242) We may sum up by saying that in regard to all the problem areas discussed here (4.5.3.1-4) we may not speak of a fundamental conflict or even opposition between justification and the church. This is quite compatible with the role of the doctrine of justification in seeing that all the church's institutions, in their self-understanding and exercise, contribute to the church's abiding in the truth of the gospel which alone in the Holy Spirit creates and sustains the church.

5. The Mission and Consummation of the Church

(243) As the recipient and mediator of salvation the church has its enduring foundation in the triune God. Its ultimate goal is consummation in God's kingdom. God will create his eternal and universal kingdom of righteousness, peace and love, and himself will bring about his own definitive reign and salvation. God has chosen and established the church by grace in this age and for this age, so that it proclaim his gospel to all creatures (cf. Mk 16:15), worship him unceasingly and praise him for the "riches of his grace" (cf. Eph 1:3-14) and in witness and service makes known to all people his loving kindness and goodness of heart (cf. Titus 3:4-6), until he himself dwells ultimately in our midst and makes all things new (cf. Rev 21:3-5). Thus while in this age the church does indeed have its responsible missionary task of proclaiming the gospel (cf. 1 Cor 9:16) and serving God and humanity (cf. Mt 22:37-40), it also goes on its way through this age in the certainty of God's mercy and grace (cf. 2 Cor 12:9) and in joyful confidence in the return of the Lord. Jesus has said to us, "But strive first for the kingdom of God and his righteousness, and all these things will be given to you as well" (Mt 6:33); and he has taught us to pray, saying "Father, hallowed be your name. Your kingdom come" (Lk 11:2).

5.1 The Church's Mission

(244) Everywhere Lutherans and Catholics find themselves repeatedly confronted by the same challenges — challenges which vary greatly in the different regions of the world and can also change very quickly (5.1.1). This leads Lutherans and Catholics to address these challenges together and to reflect afresh on the mission of the church in the light of the message of justification (5.1.2). We are agreed that our missionary task represents a true if limited participation in God's own realization of his plans as Creator, Redeemer and Sanctifier (5.1.3). Regarding the most important elements in our task

as churches — evangelization, worship and service to humanity — no essential differences divide us (5.1.4). Such a broad consensus demands of our churches that we intensify and expand their field of practical cooperation on every level in serving the gospel of Jesus Christ.

5.1.1 Common Challenges to our Churches in a Constantly Changing World

(245) The challenges facing the churches throughout the world are often quite varied, corresponding to the different regional contexts; but in a given place they confront Lutherans and Catholics and in the same way. In South Africa racist thinking has not stopped at the doors of just one church. In other countries of Africa and in parts of Asia Christians of all confessions see themselves threatened or even persecuted by a militant Islam. In the south-east part of Europe the churches face the challenge to overcome extreme ethnic and national allegiances in a situation of flagrant violation of human dignity up to genocide. In the countries of Latin America the incredible differences between poor and rich cut across all the churches and confessions. Religious alienation in the secular context of many European countries never affects only one church by itself.

(246) Many problems arise not only in the one or the other context; they confront our churches worldwide: the reawakening of nationalism, extreme rightist tendencies, increasing readiness for violence and violence itself. These and similar common challenges make the churches look afresh at their missionary task and confront them with the inescapable question, how far they can and really want to make common cause in the face of such challenges. An example of a common quest for answers to today's questions in the light of the gospel and of the various church traditions is the conciliar or ecumenical "process of mutual commitment to justice, peace and the integrity of creation" to which the Assembly of the World Council of Churches in Vancouver called in 1983. That led to the European Ecumenical Assembly "Peace with Justice" in Basel in 1989 and the "World Convocation" in Seoul in 1990, as well as to activities in many countries and regions of the world.

117

(247) How quickly contexts can change has become very clear in those countries of Eastern Europe that have in virtually bloodless revolutions liberated themselves from many years of one party's and ideology's position of supremacy. The complexity of human living conditions and the speed of social change in our age call for the churches to test constantly the challenges of the changing contexts in the light of the gospel, in order to fulfill their task of mission authentically and contextually. The "signs of the times" are thus a call to the churches to reflect on their own origins and to make appropriate responses. Together they can contribute to perceiving present forms of the enduring struggle between faith and unbelief, sin and justice, the old and the new creation, correctly. In so doing the church must pay particular attention to how people today express both their distress and their hopes.

(248) A church which has been called together by Christ to serve his work on earth will therefore always have to make an effort to realize to the utmost its missionary opportunities. The gospel message of grace and reconciliation compels those who have heard and accepted it to bring it to those who have not yet heard it or who have still had no proper opportunity to accept it. We must be alarmed when we think about those who have forgotten or estranged themselves from God's good news. Catholics and Lutherans together must accept their missionary calling as disciples of Jesus Christ. They must in common face the challenges of constant renewal in their churches under the influence of the Holy Spirit, so that they become common instruments for God's saving plan in ever more authentic ways.

(249) In reflecting on the common challenges we are fully aware of the inner relationship between church and unity. The existing separations between Lutherans and Catholics are an obstacle for the one ministry of reconciliation to which we are called. Discord among Christians openly contradicts — as Vatican II says — "the will of Christ, provides a stumbling block to the world, and inflicts damage on the most holy cause of proclaiming the good news to every creature."[340] Therefore the changing world in which we live offers a

---

[340] UR 1.

great challenge to our churches to pursue with new energy our ecumenical pilgrimage towards visible unity.

5.1.2 Reflection on the Church's Mission in Light of the Message of Justification

(250) The late prophetic testimonies of Israel already give us an inkling of a fundamental dimension of our life and calling in the church. The Lord God showed his saving power by gathering his people from the countries to which they had been dispersed and reestablishing them as his chosen servants (cf. Is 41:8-10; 43:1-7). But God's salvation is intended to reach all the ends of the earth (cf. Is 45:22f) and one day all peoples are to flock into the city of the Lord (cf. Is 60:3f,10,14). At the same time those who belong to the people of Israel are described as "witnesses" who are to testify to the mercy of the Lord and the almighty work by which he realizes his plan of salvation (cf. Is 43:10,12; 44:8). And finally some of those gathered by the Lord from different nations and tongues shall be sent to "the coastlands far away" in order to proclaim the glory of the Lord and bring new worshipers into the house of the Lord (cf. Is 66:18-21). [341]

(251) What was already in evidence in Israel in the period after the Exile reached its consummation in Jesus Christ. As church we find our identity in him, especially in his own mission to preach the gospel (cf. Mk 1:15; 1:28f), to call not the righteous but sinners (cf. Mk 2:17), and to give his life as a ransom for many (cf. Mk 10:45). Jesus found his own task of mission outlined by the prophets, to "bring good news to the poor" and "to proclaim release to the captives" (Lk 4:18); and this has continuing relevance for us as his disciples, as a guideline for our own decisions and preferences in the service of love.

(252) Jesus sent out his disciples to spread his message and healing ministry throughout Galilee (cf. Lk 9:1f). Thus at the same time he anticipated what was still to come. After his resurrection Jesus passed on his mission to the disciples, which still today is his legacy

---

[341] Cf. *Redemptoris Missio*, 12.

for Christians: "As the Father has sent me, so I send you" (Jn 20:21). In all the gospels we find this commission of the risen Lord, which defines the church. "Go into all the world and proclaim the good news to the whole creation" (Mk 16:15). "Go therefore and make disciples of all nations, baptizing them in the name of the Father and of the Son and of the Holy Spirit, and teaching them to obey everything that I have commanded you" (Mt 28:19f). "Thus it is written, that the Messiah is to suffer and to rise from the dead on the third day, and that repentance and forgiveness of sins is to be proclaimed in his name to all nations, beginning from Jerusalem" (Lk 24:46f; cf. Acts 1:8).

(253) As individuals and communities we know ourselves to be addressed by these words and in obedience we accept the commission of our Lord to evangelize, to win new disciples and to spread his healing presence throughout the world. The full significance of this commission passes our understanding. But we know that we live through him who died "to gather into one the dispersed children of God" (Jn 11:52). The church has received "fellowship ... with the Father and with his Son Jesus Christ" (1 Jn 1:3), a fellowship which is meant for all people. As the church we are chosen and destined to go out into the world and bear fruit (cf. Jn 15:16) by spreading the knowledge of the one true God and Jesus Christ, who is eternal life (cf. Jn 17:3).

(254) This call to service, so emphatically entrusted to us by the Lord, plainly exceeds our human striving and performance. The missionary sending of the church is at all times made possible by the power of the Holy Spirit, just as that power was given to the apostolic community for their witness to the risen Christ (cf. Acts 2:33-36; 3:12-15; 5:30-32; 13:1-4, 30-33). The church knows that it is filled with "power from on high" and that it is thus enabled to proclaim God's own conquest of human wickedness and his call to repentance (cf. Lk 24:47-49; Acts 2:23f). In the spirit of Pentecost the church summons men and women to baptism and to new life in congregations of apostolic teaching, to the sharing of resources and gifts, to the breaking of bread and to prayer, praise and intercession (cf. Acts 2:42-47; 4:32-35). Further evangelizing must still be carried out in our world, and our churches are confident that the Holy Spirit which was

once poured out will continue to overcome human obstacles (cf. Acts 10:44-48), open hearts to the gospel (cf. Acts 16:14) and create new congregations which are brought to life by the apostolic witness to Jesus Christ.

(255) In faith we look back on these unrepeatable beginnings through which God has deeply impressed the missionary command on the nature of the church. We bear a treasure for the world. We stand together in that ministry of reconciliation which affects the whole world. Although as individuals and communities we are only earthen vessels, we are encouraged by the Spirit of God to accept the missionary task of speaking about him in whom we believe, Jesus Christ. We have the task of preparing the ways by which he can come to human beings as their reconciler, as God's own righteousness and as the beginning of the new creation (cf. 2 Cor 5:17-21).

5.1.3 Mission as Sharing in God's Activity in the World

(256) Catholics and Lutherans are agreed that the mission of the church to proclaim the gospel and serve humanity is a true — even if also limited — sharing in God's activity in the world toward the realization of his plan as Creator, Redeemer and Sanctifier. Reflection on the nature of our calling and authority as church has priority, and we are grateful that our dialogue enables us to do this together (5.1.3.1). But God's activity in the world is more comprehensive than what he carries out through the church. And the commission to Christians to let themselves be taken by him into service goes beyond the sphere of the church. Both our traditions have developed their own ideas about this: the Lutheran doctrine of God's two kingdoms and the Catholic doctrine of the rightful autonomy of creation, [342] of earthly spheres and realities (5.1.3.2).

5.1.3.1 *Common Understanding*

(257) We have learned to understand the nature of our missionary task in the church by considering the activity of our God whom Holy

---

[342] Cf. GS 41.

Scripture reveals as Creator of heaven and earth, Redeemer of lost humanity and Sanctifier of those who are brought to the Lord Jesus Christ. Through God's grace and call, the mission of the church shares in the continuing activity of Father, Son and Holy Spirit. The church serves God's missionary activity in his world. Our ministry is therefore characterized by what we ascribe to the divine Persons, i.e., their respective activities in creation, redemption and sanctification. God graciously accepts our words and deeds by accomplishing his own plan to save and to bless.

(258) In effectual and sustaining love God the Creator is devoted to everything he has created and he shows his special love for human beings, whom he has made in his image (cf. Gen 1:26). Conversely human beings are called to be God's fellow-workers. As stewards they are entrusted with care for creation and to them is committed the promotion of justice and well-being for all, for which purpose God has given them reason and conscience as well as specific institutional structures as instruments of his creative and sustaining love. We know of course from the teaching of the faith and from our own experience that this love has to operate in the context of the fallen world which is characterized by sin. Justice and protective measures, which must be established here, can do no more than limit the effects of evil; they cannot uproot it.

(259) The call and commitment to serve God's creative and sustaining will applies to everyone, both Christians and non-Christians. They are to strive together for peace, justice and the integrity of creation. With the aid of their reason they must together look for practical ways and for a mode of organizing the institutional order which in their period of history will best serve to realize those purposes that God has appointed. Here church members have no greater competence than their non-Christian sisters and brothers who are made in the image of God; on the other hand there may be differences of opinion between them regarding the best way to achieve common objectives.

(260) In relation to the creative and sustaining will of God, church members have no additional call to obedience and no special

competence beyond that of their fellow-humans. But in view of the obscuring of the creative and sustaining will of God in this sinful world, they have a special responsibility. Transformed by the gospel, individual Christians — already a new creation in faith — have, like the church as a whole, a sharpened awareness of the standards and tasks that hold good for all human beings, and advocate them with unprejudiced hearts. Where necessary, vis a vis other persons as well as on their behalf, Christians are to step in both by admonition, advice and action and by their own style of life in the cause of human dignity, fundamental human rights, and for freedom, justice and the integrity of creation. They are to alleviate distress and suffering. Thus as individuals and as a church community they point to God-given values and standards of creation. At the same time they draw the attention of their fellow-creatures to the limited objectives and possibilities of their social and political activities and preserve them from excessive ideological demands and from the temptation to totalitarianism.

(261) God sent the Son as Redeemer in order to proclaim unconditional divine grace for sinful humanity. In the form of a servant Jesus took sin upon himself in order to conquer it and make available to all believers a share of his righteousness, and of new life and access to the Father in the Holy Spirit. Jesus Christ is the center of the missionary task of the church, which recognizes that he has commissioned it to bring his liberating message and grace to all peoples. Here lies the special mission of the church: to fulfill Jesus' commission, to missionize the world and to build up communities of disciples who, transformed by faith already here on earth, radiate the firm hope of future fulfillment of the kingdom of God on the day of eschatological consummation. Church members rejoice in their regeneration through baptism, in which they have been anointed in Christ through the Holy Spirit to be members of a priestly, prophetic and royal people. From baptism they receive their supreme dignity and their responsibility to serve the mission of Jesus Christ in dependence on him and conformed to him. This includes the priestly ministry of praise, self-sacrifice and intercession. Part of this is the prophetic commission to expose evil, proclaim salvation and also witness to the hope of glory in the midst of the afflictions of this age. Royal dignity is therein

epitomized by living in Christian freedom from sin and from the contrarieties of the world (cf. Rom 8:31-39), and thus serving humanity fearlessly by word and deed, so that the dominion of sin will be overcome, creation will serve human welfare and preferential love will be shown to our weak and ill-treated brothers and sisters.

(262) God sent the Spirit into the world to bring people to faith by means of word and sacrament, to justify sinners and to call together the church as a *koinonia*, in this way attaining the ends of the mission of the Son. Thus in the midst of the old world the new creation is already raised up in holiness. In baptism, through the Spirit, men and women are made members of a community which acts as instrument of the Spirit's mission. Through proclamation in different forms, through actions which testify to the new world which has dawned — though still marked by ambiguity and limitation — and, where necessary, through acting representatively and critically for the present world, Christians implement this task and thus minister to the saving rule of God which has already begun with the death and resurrection of Jesus and with the outpouring of the Holy Spirit.

5.1.3.2 *Two Traditions*

(263) Lutherans and Catholics understand the mission of the church as sharing in God's activity in the world; they also know, however, that God's activity in the world goes beyond the sphere of the church. Even if bounds are set to the God-given task of the church, Christians are aware that they must serve God in all areas of society. How this is understood and practiced is differently expressed in our two traditions.

5.1.3.2.1 The Lutheran Teaching on the Two Kingdoms

(264) In order to do justice theologically and pastorally to this situation, the Lutheran tradition developed the doctrine of the "two kingdoms (realms)" of God. This is not a concrete socioethical program, but it does define an ethical *locus* for Christians who already live their lives as citizens of the new world while also continuing as citizens of the old world. How can Christians, whose rule of life is the Sermon on the Mount, hold responsible positions in politics,

administration of justice, law enforcement, economy or the military? The two kingdoms cannot be equated with the distinction between the church and the world; they are also to be found within the church, because the church is a *corpus permixtum* and every Christian is still a sinner.

(265) The real life-context of Christians is the spiritual kingdom of the *communio sanctorum*. Here Christ is head of a spiritual realm, as through word and sacrament in the Holy Spirit he brings people to faith and preserves that faith.[343] The behavior appropriate to this kingdom is the radical love that corresponds to the Sermon on the Mount,[344] a love that arises out of faith and is made possible by the Holy Spirit: unreserved readiness to serve, waiving one's own rights, non-resistance, non-violence in following Jesus Christ and in his strength. Such love makes visible already in the present world the new world desired by God.

(266) Because this love is the fruit of the heart transformed in faith, it cannot be elevated to the status of law nor advocated as a general standard for social life. Indeed in the context of the fallen world that would mean giving evil the upper hand and handing over human society to the selfishness and arbitrariness of the powerful.[345] Where faith does not prevail, that is, among non-Christians, but also in regard to Christians themselves, since they too remain sinners, it is necessary to have a social order which checks evil, and which despite evil guarantees the best possible life. This will be an order which cares for the protection of life and limb and for civic justice.[346] Its instruments are not the word and the Spirit but the law[347] and institutions which are equipped with power and make use of force where there is no other possibility.[348] The social order does not operate through the transformation of hearts but by imposing obliga-

---

[343] Apol 16; BC 222ff; cf. also CA 28,8f; LC III, 53.
[344] LC I, 5th Commandment; BC 390f; WA 6,36f,43; 15,300f; 11,245,250; 30/II,111f.
[345] WA 15,302; 11,252f; cf. Apol 16,6.
[346] CA 28,11.
[347] *usus civilis legis*.
[348] CA 28,11.

tions and calling for obedience, and in the last resort through compulsion.

(267) Although this ordering of life does not correspond to God's real intentions for humanity it is nevertheless also an instrument of his love, as his "worldly kingdom," through which he preserves and forms creation even in its fallen state. Such ordering of life must therefore be affirmed as "instituted and ordained by God for the sake of good order."[349] As distinct from the spiritual kingdom the instruments of the worldly kingdom are not contingently and particularly effectual, rather its standards are embedded in the consciences of human beings[350] and established in the institutions of human society.[351] That is to say, they can and must claim universality and prove themselves in human society. Consequently the actual structuring of political and social life is entrusted in great measure to human reason and expertise, whether of Christians or non-Christians,[352] and may vary according to context and historical perspective.[353] All structuring possibilities aim at and are limited by the contribution they make to the preservation and just ordering of the world.

(268) The two kingdoms have to be strictly distinguished with regard to their goals, instruments and methods.[354] If this does not happen, either the spiritual kingdom is robbed of its uniqueness, as the renewed heart and corresponding ethic of radical love and renunciation are reduced to conventional morality and sociopolitical justice, or conversely the worldly kingdom is ruined. It is ruined because society, thinking its members are already wholly good, dispenses with erecting the barriers of external order, laws and needed institutional force against evil and thus leaves the field open for it, or because the attempt is made to influence hearts and achieve unselfish, idealistic acts — by whatever criteria one measures these — with the use of compulsion.

[349] CA 16; BC 37; cf. Apol 13,15; BC 213.
[350] FC SD 5; BC 564ff.
[351] LC I, 141f; 150; BC 384ff.
[352] WA 40,III,221-223.
[353] WA 18,818; 24,6-9.
[354] CA 28,12; BC 83; Apol 16,2; BC 222.

(269) Nevertheless, distinguishing between the two kingdoms does not mean separating them. They cannot be parceled out between two separate groups as if the renewed heart and its corresponding ethic were something for only a few, while the mass of Christians could do without them. Rather they are given with faith itself and are common to all Christians. [355] But all Christians continue to be also citizens of the unredeemed world and as creatures of God together with all other human beings they have the responsibility of caring for its preservation and organization and of committing themselves to serving God's worldly kingdom. Thus Christians, according to their respective station in society (one's "calling") will also hold and exercise power, help in promoting and enforcing law, and put down violence — even by the use of disciplined opposing force — instead of renouncing power, law and force in the spirit of the Sermon on the Mount. [356] Whether they act in the one way or the other depends on whether they are acting on their own behalf or for others. Here the spheres frequently overlap so that Christians can decide which principle they must follow according to their own consciences only. But they can be certain that even where because of societal responsibility they exercise or appeal to power, law and force they are not contradicting God's will but serving it. [357] Indeed they have to regard this service as a duty in the practical and disinterested fulfillment of which they demonstrate their Christianity in the world. [358] In such activity, even if they do nothing other than is done by all persons of good will, they will do it differently, by bringing into evidence something of the love and readiness to forgive which is a special characteristic of Christian faith. [359] But they will also be aware of working to preserve and order a world in which evil still lurks and sets limits to the good that may be achieved.

(270) In contrast to the sixteenth century, the doctrine of the two kingdoms requires modification in many respects today. For historical

---

[355] LC I; BC 390f; WA 6,37f; 11,245,249f; 18,308f.
[356] Apol 15,25f; BC 218f.
[357] Apol 16,13; BC 224.
[358] CA 27,49; BC 78f; Apol 27,37; BC 275.
[359] Apol 4,121f; BC 124; cf. also WA 11,279; 7,544f, 600; 15,293.

changes and the unsettled nature of social structures, with the resultant opportunities and difficulties, are more obvious today than before. Also the fact that justice and the ironing out of social inequalities — not only among individuals but also among groups, nations and continents — is perceived in an entirely different way today, as memoranda and other church statements of the last few decades show. But all this does not change anything in the fundamental assertions of the doctrine of God's two kingdoms itself. It continues to show the way by making it possible to maintain the eschatological existence of believers but at the same time to assert their place and responsibility for the world, which remains God's creation but is still unredeemed, without the two spheres being confused or separated.

(271) Thus on the one hand the doctrine of the two kingdoms secures that the life of faith has another foundation, other instruments and another shape than sociopolitical life in the world. Neither are worldly authorities entitled to intervene in spiritual concerns, nor can faith and its ethical fruits become worldly themselves by becoming a social program, whether utopian or of a clerical and theocratic nature. And on the other hand it makes clear that the conservation and ordering of the world, even in its unredeemed state, are subordinate to the will of God, but that this is to be worked out in ways which are not specifically Christian and comprehensible only to believers, but which claim to apply for everyone. Thus the doctrine of the two kingdoms makes it possible to allow autonomy in sociopolitical actions over against the gospel and to endorse the secular character of the ordinances of the world — though this autonomy may not set itself against God's purpose of conserving and properly ordering the world. Those who are aware that ethical standards are based in the will of God must be especially vigilant in insisting on this, in view of the manifold obscuring elements in the life of society. The doctrine of the two kingdoms imposes on Christians a life and activity in tension between two systems of reference, but this is the same tension present in the very nature of the life of faith, that of being in the world and not of the world. This tension will be resolved only with the full and definitive dawn of the kingdom of God.

5.1.3.2.2 The Roman Catholic Teaching on the "Proper Autonomy of Earthly Affairs"

(272) Catholic teaching also recognizes the limits of the church's task, especially by its acknowledgment of the proper "autonomy of earthly affairs."[360] This autonomy does not leave human activities in the political and economic fields to arbitrary decisions. But neither can these fields be directly explained or shaped by the biblical revelation and the gospel of Jesus Christ. The Catholic view of autonomy rests on the perception that the Creator has endowed all his creatures with their own specific nature and inner development, with their own structures, values and modes of action. Human experience, studies and rational reflections are entitled to explore creation. Moreover the values which permeate this world impinge on the human moral conscience on all levels.

(273) Reason and conscience operate together in molding the order of this world. Nevertheless Christian faith places the realities of the world in a new horizon of meaning and integrates them there. Christian values, such as the dignity and freedom of each person as well as mercy, kindness and gentleness in social legislation, are to be integrated into responsibility for the world. Therefore faith makes it possible to challenge critically destructive tendencies in society, politics, economics and culture and to strengthen the positive impulses of a secular ethic.

(274) "Christ, to be sure, gave His Church no proper mission in the political, economic or social order. The purpose which he set before her is a religious one."[361] He commissioned his disciples to spread his gospel, build up congregations, promote holiness and guide people to eternal life. These religious priorities free the church from any essential ties with a particular form of human culture or a specific political, economic or social system. The church lays claim to no power over the secular sphere no matter how much it strives for the freedom to operate in society, to serve selflessly and to testify to Christ's message. Catholic doctrine addresses Christians as "citizens

[360] GS 36.
[361] GS 42.

of two cities" and reminds them of the profusion of their professional, political and social duties.[362] Calling people to action in this world is in fact stimulated by Christ's call to conversion and newness of life. Christian formation stimulates new energies and a new sensitivity which are discernibly advantageous to the secular world. It promotes, for example, a vision of unity which transcends all differences of nationality, race and class, a detachment from possessions as the standard of personal dignity and a dynamic of love for humanity for whose salvation Christ died.

(275) On the basis of new social, political and economic challenges in the last two centuries, challenges which did not previously exist, Catholic theology has developed a social teaching which to a great extent has been received magisterially. This teaching of the popes, the Second Vatican Council and numerous bishops' conferences is primarily directed towards molding the moral conscience of church members but is also concerned with persuading all people of good will and thus influencing public order. This socioethical doctrine has developed, and will go on developing, in the effort to keep pace with the rapid changes in the modern industrial world and the gap between North and South. By nature it is a doctrine regarding human beings in society, human dignity, human rights and the moral values that must determine social action. Pope and bishops have not flinched from denouncing systematic exploitation and injustice. The same socioethical doctrine has however refrained from offering ready-made models and promoting the implementation of technical solutions for problems. It has left open the field where rational research and personal values converge as the basis of options for the creation of a social order. It is even officially acknowledged that within the church there can be differences of opinion between honest and faithful Catholics in regard to their individual modes of procedure in the promotion of the common good.[363]

(276) This comprehensive body of social teaching, whose individual statements are issued with different degrees of binding charac-

---

[362] GS 43.
[363] Cf. GS 43.

ter, represents an aspect in contemporary Catholic life and teaching to which, for the theological reasons explained above, nothing in the Lutheran churches corresponds. At a future stage in our dialogue this aspect of asymmetry between our churches must be dealt with in regard to socioethical questions and, more fundamentally, in relation to the extent of the church's competence in moral questions.

5.1.4 The Fundamental Components of the Church's Missionary Task

(277) Lutherans and Catholics are agreed on the priority of the task of evangelizing the world (5.1.4.1), on the central significance of proclaiming and celebrating the grace of God in worship (5.1.4.2) and on the commandment to serve humanity as a whole (5.1.4.3). They also agree that "*martyria, leitourgia* and *diakonia* (witness, worship and service to the neighbor) are tasks entrusted to the whole people of God."[364]

5.1.4.1 *Commission to Evangelize*

(278) The essential task which our Lord gave his church is the proclamation of the good news of his saving death and his resurrection. As Christians we share in the Lord's missionary commission and, like the apostolic preaching on the Day of Pentecost, our message too contains the invitation to baptism and to sharing in the promised Spirit of new life and freedom (cf. Acts 2:38). We are convinced that evangelism brings with it God's unique gift of grace to the world and we agree with the words of the Apostle Paul, "...woe to me if I do not proclaim the gospel!" (1 Cor 9:16).

(279) Evangelism lays claim to the whole person for witness to Christ; it demands the witness of a life which corresponds to the gospel in faith, hope and love. Here it is not simply a question of the work done by those sent out as missionaries but also of the witness of each individual Christian and each Christian community. Although the specific objective of evangelizing is bringing people to faith and not creating a new order of society, it nevertheless has a profound

[364] *The Ministry in the Church*, 13.

effect on the life of society. For Christians today insist on the strict observation of freedom of religion and freedom of conscience, and in common with all people of good will they are especially watchful and zealous in supporting the conservation and humane structuring of the world, and enter the lists against discrimination, oppression and injustice. By the way in which they do these things, they make evident the love and forgiveness of God that has been bestowed on them.

(280) We recognize that it is particularly necessary nowadays to enter into inter-religious dialogue, paying respectful heed to those who belong to other religious traditions. It is imperative to respect the convictions of others in order to create a basis for peace in societies where Christians live as neighbors of adherents of other great world religions. We keep ourselves open to the idea that God can be active in hidden ways in non-Christian religions too, and we therefore enter into dialogue with other religions in a trusting readiness to learn. Beyond such dialogue, however, we also see ourselves as obliged by the gospel to bear credible witness to the grace and truth which have been given to the whole world in a unique way in Jesus Christ, and we hope that this witness encounters faith.

(281) In our day a special task is the re-evangelizing of tradition-ally Christian areas where large numbers of the baptized have lapsed into mere nominal Christianity. We are thus commissioned to invite our contemporaries to recognize afresh the glory of God that shines in the face of Jesus and to accept the message of reconciliation (cf. 2 Cor 4:6; 5:19). A precious treasure has been entrusted to us which we should pass on to all people.

5.1.4.2 Centrality of Worship

(282) Our dialogue has already expressed a common understand-ing of our calling to join in the great eucharistic doxology in the presence of our Lord: "through him, with him, in him in the unity of the Holy Spirit all honor and glory is yours, almighty Father now and forever." For our unity with Christ leads to the everlasting Father through the power of the Holy Spirit in preaching, thanksgiving and

praise, intercession and self-offering. [365] Worship is thus central to our mission as a church, for in it we celebrate our justification in Christ and proclaim as a priestly people the marvelous works of him who has called us "out of darkness into his marvelous light" (1 Pet 2:9).

(283) Common worship is by its nature not a means to any other end. Worship is rather the most important matrix of faith and an essential expression of it, for in worship our faith is induced and nourished through the proclamation of the gospel of Christ and our common sharing with others in the same gospel and the same sacramental life. In worship we are linked with Christians of every age right back to the apostles and joyfully celebrate the grace of communion with the Father and his Son Jesus Christ (cf. 1 Jn 1:3). Worship may therefore never be made to serve an ideology or be reduced to an educational tool. Services of worship are intended to attract and invite people and to radiate an aura of the kindness and benevolence of our God, who has redeemed us because of his mercy (cf. Titus 3:4-6).

(284) In worship our church community, the church at a particular time and in a particular place, becomes concrete and visible in a special way. The annual round of the liturgical seasons and feasts, with their climaxes at Christmas, Good Friday/Easter and Pentecost, deepens our ecclesial identity as the people of God, the body of Christ and the temple of the Holy Spirit. When we gather together to confess our sins, to hear God's saving word, to remember his great deeds, and to sing hymns and songs, to intercede for a blessing on everyone and to celebrate the eucharistic meal, we are a people of faith in the most pregnant sense. This is our proper task as church, and we accept it as such with a sense of responsibility to offer our Creator and Redeemer adoration and praise in the name of all creatures, through our Lord Christ. In worship the existence of the church as an existence for others becomes particularly clear in "supplications, prayers, intercessions, and thanksgivings" (1 Tim 2:1f) for all people, particularly also for those responsible in government, which the congregation assembled in the Holy Spirit in the presence of Christ offers to God. Here

---

[365] *The Eucharist*, 12; 29-37.

too we must remain aware that as justified sinners we ourselves are constantly in need of repentance and conversion. Since we have been called to such a ministry of reconciliation we lament all the more the scandal of separation and the divisions among us, which are an obstacle to the full expression of the unity of the one priestly people that comes before God to praise him and be renewed through his word and Spirit.

5.1.4.3 Responsibility of the Church and the Service of Humanity

(285) Our task must bear the deep imprint of Jesus' view: "For the Son of Man came not to be served but to serve, and to give his life a ransom for many" (Mk 10:45). In following him, who in "the form of a slave" (Phil 2:7) became the mediator of the grace we have received, we have been called to an attitude and behavior like his. In obedience to him who affirmed the Creator's will for the world, we must contribute to its preservation and well-being. Thus as Christians and as communities we are instruments of God in the service of mercy and justice in the world.

(286) God's activity in the world is more comprehensive than what he does through the church. Fulfilling the commission of evangelism and worship is the service due to all humanity. By striving in common with all people of good will for healing, protection and promotion of human dignity, for respectful and rational handling of the resources of creation, for the consolidation of social unity, respect for social diversity and for deepening of the general sense of responsibility, Christians are servants of the Creator's love for the world. Through their readiness to do without and their unselfish charity they reflect the light of Christ even where his name is not confessed.

(287) Together with their non-Christian brothers and sisters, but also where necessary over against them, Christians serve humanity by championing human dignity and inalienable and inviolable human rights. Knowing that these are received by human beings from their Creator, the church interprets them as expressions of an obligation toward God and speaks to others of the transcendent dimension of their lives. If necessary, the church also must address specific

political and social problems in the effort to raise consciousness regarding human distress and the demands of civil justice.

(288) Christians serve human society by supporting structures in politics, law, administration, education and economics which promote holistic human development. They contribute towards awareness and the strengthening of ties that bind all human beings in one family despite racial, cultural, national and socioeconomic differences. They are eager to provide generous aid in situations of special distress, and they work on projects directed towards promoting long-term solutions to overcome misery.

(289) The contribution which Christians make in all areas of social life — in politics, education and nurture, health, science, culture and the mass media — is to work like yeast in dough. Such action, determined by competence and dedication, is an essential part of the task which Christians are to fulfill in order to stop the destructive flood of evil and to promote lives in accord with human dignity and reverence toward God.

5.2 The Eschatological Consummation of the Church

(290) Reflection on the church as the recipient and mediator of salvation as well as on its mission would remain incomplete if its eschatological consummation were not also taken into account. It is precisely in the eschatological consummation of the church, as seen by the New Testament and expressed in the creed, that we see the convergence in God of all the paths of the church as God's pilgrim people. God himself definitively causes his rule and his salvation to prevail. Thus the church's role as recipient and mediator of salvation once again becomes plain in terms of its end and consummation. In what follows, the eschatological consummation of the church will be considered from a twofold standpoint: first, in regard to the communion of saints (*sanctorum communio*) as it is confessed in the Apostles' Creed (5.2.1), and second, in regard to the New Testament message of the kingdom and rule of God (5.2.2).

5.2.1   Sanctorum Communio

5.2.1.1   Common Faith

(291) Lutherans and Catholics confess "the communion of saints" (*sanctorum communionem*) in the Apostles' Creed. According to Luther's Large Catechism this means the church: a "Christian congregation or assembly," "a holy Christian people." It is a communion of saints because it lives harmoniously in one faith and in love under one head, Christ, and by the Holy Spirit. Through the Holy Spirit every member of this "holy community" shares in everything and especially in the word of God. The Holy Spirit constantly remains with the church, sanctifies it, strengthens its faith and produces its fruits. [366]

(292) The *Catechismus Romanus* understands the expression *sanctorum communio* similarly as the explanation of what the church is, for communion "with the Father and with his Son Jesus Christ" is realized in this community of the saints (1 Jn 1:3). "Communion of saints" means communion on the basis of the confession of faith and the sacraments, especially baptism and the eucharist, and on the basis of the interrelationship of all members of the body of Christ. It is a unity and community brought about by the Spirit, because the Holy Spirit sees to it that whatever gift anyone has belongs to the whole communion. [367]

(293) Catholics and Lutherans confess in common that the "communion of saints" is the community of those united in sharing in the word and sacraments (the *sancta*) in faith through the Holy Spirit, the community of "those who are sanctified in Christ Jesus [and] called to be saints [the *sancti*]" (1 Cor 1:2).

5.2.1.2   Community of Perfected Saints

(294) Beyond the circle of believers in Christ who live on earth, the "communion of saints" is seen as a community of those who have been sanctified, cutting across all the ages and reaching into the

---

[366] Cf. LC II,3; BC 417ff.
[367] Cf. *The Catechism of the Council of Trent*, I:X,23-26.

eternity of God, a community in which one shares and into which one enters through the church. The patristic church believed "the communion of saints" to the glory of God, honored God himself in the saints and thus kept alive the longing for the life to come. In the Lutheran Confessions too there is a fundamental adherence to the idea of a living communion with the saints, for despite criticism of invocation of the saints it is not denied that we should give "honor to the saints:" in thanks to God for their gifts of grace, in the strengthening of our faith because of their example and in "imitation, first of their faith and then of their other virtues, which each should imitate in accordance with his calling."[368] It is granted "that the angels pray for us" and that "the saints in heaven pray for the church."[369] From ancient times therefore in the preface of the liturgy it is said: "Through him the angels praise your majesty, the heavenly hosts adore you, and the powers tremble; together with the blessed Seraphim all the citizens of heaven praise you in brilliant jubilation. Unite our voices with theirs and let us sing praise in endless adoration: Holy, holy, holy."[370] Vatican II placed the ideas of the Fathers and the practice of venerating the saints in an ecclesiological context.[371] It stresses the eschatological character of the church as the pilgrim people of God and speaks of that people's "union with the Church in heaven."[372]

5.2.1.3 Communion of the Church on Earth with the Perfected Saints

(295) In confessing the *sanctorum communio* our common faith in the triune God who will perfect the church finds expression. For the *communio* with God which has already been given and realized on earth through Jesus Christ in the Holy Spirit is the foundation of Christian hope beyond death and of the *communio* between Christ's saints on earth and Christ's saints who have already died. The communion of saints reaches beyond death because it is founded in God himself. Only through death and judgment can individuals and

---

[368] Apol 21,4-7; BC 229f.
[369] Apol 21,8f; BC 230.
[370] *The Eucharist*, 39.
[371] Cf. LG 50f.
[372] LG 50.

the church as a whole reach consummation (cf. 1 Cor 4:4f; 2 Cor 5:10; Acts 10:42; Heb 11:6; 9:27; 1 Pet 4:17). Thus belief in the communion of saints as the consummation of the church in no way makes light of sin, death and judgment. Because our fellowship with the dead is in God alone, our relations with the dead are in the safe keeping of the mystery of God. Such an unfathomable difference exists between the present temporal and the future eternal life (cf. 1 Cor 15:37-57) that we cannot adequately comprehend eternal life in words. We can express it only in images of hope, as Holy Scripture indicates (cf. 1 Cor 2:9). Nevertheless we believe in the fundamental indestructibility of the life given us in Christ through the power of the Holy Spirit even through the judgment and beyond death.

(296) Because of the horror of death we mourn the dead at the grave, but because we are Christians we mourn as those who have hope. Our common Christian hope is the crucified and risen Lord through whom God will also lead the dead to glory with Christ (cf. 1 Thess 4:14). Those who are sanctified in Christ Jesus will be "with the Lord forever" (1 Thess 4:17) even through death and judgment. Christians believe in God, who is not a God of the dead but of the living (cf. Mk 12:27 par), for "to him all of them are alive" (Lk 20:38b). Paul confesses that we do not live or die to ourselves but that "whether we live or whether we die, we are the Lord's" (Rom 14:7-9) and that nothing, not even death, can separate us "from the love of God in Christ Jesus our Lord" (Rom 8:35-39). Therefore the pilgrim people of God are aware that they look "for the city that is to come" (Heb 13:14) of the sanctified church, "the heavenly Jerusalem, ... the assembly of the firstborn who are enrolled in heaven, ... and to the spirits of the righteous made perfect" (Heb 12:22f). The communion of saints, the unity of the pilgrim and heavenly church, is realized especially in worship, in the adoration and praise of the thrice-holy God and the Lamb, our Lord Jesus Christ (cf. Rev 4:2-11; 5:9-14). The pilgrim church reaches its goal and thus its end and consummation when "the last enemy ... death" is deprived of its power and the Son hands over everything to the rule of God the Father so that "God may be all in all" (1 Cor 15:24-28).

5.2.2   The Church and the Kingdom of God

5.2.2.1   *New Testament View*

(297) According to the witness of the Synoptic Gospels the reign of God is the core of the preaching of Jesus of Nazareth (cf. Mk 1:15; Mt 4:17), the petition for the coming of his Father's kingdom is the center and fulcrum of his prayer (cf. Lk 11:2; Mt 6:9f) and the reign of God comes to human beings as the reality proclaimed as well by his deeds (cf. Lk 11:20; Mt 12:28). Thus through and in Jesus himself the reign of God becomes present, and thus God's Lordship establishes itself among those whom Jesus healed and who were affected by his preaching (cf. Lk 17:20f).

(298) By his preaching and practice of the kingdom of God Jesus wished to call all Israel and prepare them to be eschatologically renewed and recreated by God. Especially the calling and sending out of the twelve (cf. Mk 3:14; 6:7 and Mt 10:6) is a luminous sign that the reign of God presumes an actual people, in and through whom that kingdom can be established. The coming of the kingdom of God and the eschatological new creation of Israel belong inseparably together. Right up to his death Jesus maintained this, as shown by the eschatological perspective of his eucharistic words (cf. Mk 14:25 par; Lk 13:29; 14:15; 22:30). Jesus' last meal, as an anticipation and interpretation of his death, becomes a bequest ensuring that God's offer is renewed for all Israel through Jesus' death as an atonement. Without merit or limit sins are forgiven and new life bestowed (cf. Mk 14:24 par).

(299) Even if God has created for himself in the church an actual people made up of Jews and Gentiles (cf. Eph 2:11-22) who owe their existence to the death and resurrection of Jesus and to the sending of the Spirit, this "new" people of God, which believes in the Messiah as having come, is still fundamentally related to Israel as a whole. The will of Jesus to gather Israel together held good then and still does. Seen in this way, Jesus' will to gather the eschatological people of God in wholeness and fullness, and under the rule of God, already includes the post-Easter church. Paul confirms this in his reflections

on Israel in relation to salvation-history: in the church consisting of Jews and Gentiles it is specifically the Gentile Christians who must never forget the origin of salvation-history. Israel became salvation to the nations and will also be saved (cf. Rom 9-11). For the church this means that it is the actual people of God in whom the reign of God is already kindled and through whom it is to extend. The church is the dawning and the sign of the kingdom of God.

5.2.2.2 Lutheran View

(300) Though the Lutheran Confessions contain no specific reflections on the theme of the kingdom of God and the church, there are nevertheless enough indications that the church is oriented towards the kingdom of God and taken into service for that kingdom, and that hidden in the church the kingdom of God or of Christ has already dawned and is at work. In the explanation of the second petition in the Lord's Prayer the *Large Catechism* equates the kingdom of God with the saving activity of Jesus Christ who was sent "into the world to redeem and deliver us from the power of the devil and to bring us to himself and rule us as a king of righteousness, life and salvation." This he does in the Holy Spirit through his word. This kingdom is a "kingdom of grace" which is already actively present here on earth but will be consummated in eternity and will bring its citizens to their destination there. Coming to us temporally "through the Word and faith" it will become manifest "in eternity" and definitively on the return of Christ. [373]

(301) According to the Apology the church is the kingdom of Christ as the *congregatio sanctorum*, as he rules by the word and by preaching, works through the Holy Spirit and increases in us faith, the fear of God, love and patience within the heart. [374] The church is not identical with the ultimate and all-embracing kingdom which God will introduce at the end of the ages but in the church it already begins here on earth [375] and is already hiddenly present. [376] In good works as fruit

[373] LC III,51ff; BC 426f.
[374] Apol. 16,54; BC 222ff.
[375] *Ibid.*
[376] Apol 7,17; BC 171.

of faith it is already visible before the whole world. [377] In itself, however, the kingdom is "hidden under the cross," like Jesus before he entered his heavenly dominion. [378] Mingled with unbelievers (cf. Mt 13:36ff,47ff; 25:1ff) and still sinners themselves, the holy members of the church cannot yet represent the kingdom of God unambiguously. In spite of the fact that the church is not a "Platonic republic," [379] the kingdom has already broken in. Only the *notae*, the marks of the church, i.e., the "pure teaching of the Gospel and the sacraments" are unequivocal. This tension will cease only when at the end of the ages Christ himself totally realizes and reveals the kingdom. [380]

5.2.2.3 *Catholic View*

(302) Catholics are also persuaded that the kingdom of God is inseparably linked with the person of Jesus Christ. "In Christ's word, in His works and in His presence this kingdom reveals itself to men." [381] In Jesus the reign of God has dawned and he himself is the reign of God in person. The Council speaks in a more nuanced way about the church. On the one hand it says that it receives from the exalted Lord "the mission to proclaim and to establish among all peoples the kingdom of Christ and of God," but on the other hand it stresses that despite its gradual growth the church "strains toward the consummation of the kingdom." [382] Its destiny is "the kingdom of God which has been begun by God Himself on earth, and which is to be further extended until it is brought to perfection by Him at the end of time. Then Christ our life (cf. Col 3:4) will appear." [383] In this way the Council clearly highlights the church's being taken into service for the kingdom of God and on the other hand keeps open, in the eschatological reservation, the fact that the kingdom of God is not at human disposal. God himself will establish and perfect his reign. The church

---

[377] Apol 4,189; BC 133.
[378] Apol 7:18f; BC 171; see above 142f.
[379] Apol 7,20; BC 171; "*civitas platonica.*"
[380] Apol 7,17-20; BC 171.
[381] LG 5.
[382] *Ibid.*
[383] LG 9.

is only "the kingdom of Christ now present in mystery,"[384] the "initial budding forth of that kingdom" on earth.[385]

(303) Thus, taking up the sacramental ecclesiological thinking of the Council, one can also speak of the church as the sacramental sign of the kingdom of God through the presence of the Lord in the Holy Spirit.[386] Because the crucified and risen Lord is with his church "always, to the end of the age" (Mt 28:20), it is — with trust in this promise — the sacramental sign of the kingdom of God. The presence of the Lord is made actual in the Holy Spirit and is communicated in the word of God, the celebration of the eucharist and the other sacraments, and in the community of brothers and sisters. The Spirit does indeed "blow where it chooses" (Jn 3:8) but in and through the church this Spirit accomplishes the saving activity of God and his reign. The Spirit works in the world in the witness and service of the church and in the Spirit the church fulfills its adoration, its intercessions and its advocacy for everyone before God. Thus the church serves the reign of God for the world. It is directed towards the kingdom of God as its eschatological salvation.

(304) The kingdom of God is therefore the church's constant orientation, abiding motivation, critical court of appeal and final goal. The power of the coming kingdom is already really present in the church through its Lord in the Holy Spirit. The Holy Spirit effects forgiveness of sins, sanctification and life in the church. The Spirit supports its mission and perfects its catholicity. In the miracle of tongues at Pentecost the "divisiveness of Babel" is indeed fundamentally overcome.[387] Nevertheless the Spirit makes the church repeatedly cry, Come! so that the dispersed children of God may ultimately be gathered together (cf. Rev 22:17-20; Jn 11:52). Seen in this way, the church is the place where the reign of God has already dawned, and thus it is the recipient of salvation. But at the same time it is also an instrument and sign for the reign which God himself implements, and thus it is the mediator of salvation. At the end the

[384] LG 3.
[385] LG 5.
[386] See above 121-125.
[387] AG 4.

142

church will be taken up into the kingdom of God, i.e., it will come to an end because it is no longer needed as sign and instrument. But this end is also the consummation of its earthly form as the place of God's reign and the beginning of its new, definitive existence in the eternal kingdom of God. [388]

5.2.2.4 Perspective in Ecumenical Dialogue

(305) In ecumenical dialogue too the church is seen in various ways as sign and instrument of the presence of Christ, the mission of Christ and the kingdom. Thus the Commission on Faith and Order of the World Council of Churches states that "the Church is called to be a visible sign of the presence of Christ, who is both hidden and revealed to faith, reconciling and healing human alienation in the worshipping community." [389] In its report on the meeting in Bangalore the same Commission says, "The Church is a sign and instrument of Christ's mission to all humankind." [390] In the message of the 1980 World Conference on Mission and Evangelism in Melbourne it was said that "the good news of the kingdom must be presented to the world by the church, the Body of Christ, the sacrament of the kingdom in every place and time." [391] Despite all the inadequacies of the churches as they actually exist, the reality of their character as signs of the eschatological rule of God is highlighted and stressed: "Yet there is reality here. The whole church of God, in every place and time, is a sacrament of the kingdom which came in the person of Jesus Christ and will come in its fulness when he returns in glory." [392]

(306) Similar pronouncements are to be found in the bilateral ecumenical dialogues. Thus in the Lutheran-Roman Catholic dialogue in the USA the mission of the church is seen "to be an anticipatory and efficacious sign of the final unification of all things when God will be

---

[388] Cf. LG 48f.
[389] *Uniting in Hope. Accra 1974*, 93, Faith and Order Paper 72.
[390] *Sharing in One Hope. Bangalore 1978*, 239, Faith and Order Paper 92.
[391] *Your Kingdom Come*, World Council of Churches, Geneva, 1980, 235f.
[392] *Ibid.*

all in all." [393] The Anglican-Lutheran dialogue calls the church "an instrument for proclaiming and manifesting God's sovereign rule and saving grace," [394] but also indicates that an "authentic fellowship of the reconciled" [395] is a precondition for the proper exercise of the mission and service of the church. Thus a necessary reservation is pointed out in order to evaluate realistically talk of the church as a sign of the kingdom of God. It is an ongoing task of the church to be a credible sign of the kingdom. Its credibility will repeatedly be distorted by human weakness and sin and become blurred by lack of contrition. Therefore the church always needs purification through repentance and renewal. The Report of Section III of the World Conference on Mission and Evangelism in Melbourne speaks of a frightening claim, "frightening, because it causes everyone of us to examine our personal experience of the empirical church and to confess how often our church life has hidden rather than revealed the sovereignty of God the Father whom Jesus Christ made known." [396]

5.2.2.5 Common Witness

(307) Lutherans and Catholics together regard the church as the dawning and the instrument of the kingdom of God. Two things should be maintained together. On the one hand there is the reality of the powers of the kingdom of God, especially in the proclamation of the word of God and the celebration of the sacraments as the means of salvation, but also in the reconciled community of sisters and brothers as the place of salvation. On the other hand there is the interim nature of all words and signs in which salvation is imparted, but also the inadequacies in preaching, worship and the serving community as these exist in practice among believers. To this extent the church always lives on the basis of letting itself be lifted up into the coming kingdom, remembering its own provisional nature. The earthly church will find its eschatological consummation only when the

---

[393] "Differing Attitudes Toward Papal Primacy" 1, in: *Papal Primacy and the Universal Church*, Minneapolis, 1974.

[394] Anglican-Lutheran International Conversations, London, 1973 (Pullach Report), 59 in *Growth in Agreement*, 13-34.

[395] Ibid.

[396] *Your Kingdom Come*, 193.

kingdom has come. Then when God's kingdom dawns the church will be consummated and all hiddenness fully revealed.

(308) The assembly of the faithful as a community of the perfected is the consummation of the church in the unveiled, pure presence and reign of God who is love, with whom and in whom all those made perfect have community and are in constant touch with each other: "God may be all in all" (1 Cor 15:24-28). "And I heard a loud voice from the throne saying, 'See, the home of God is among mortals. He will dwell with them as their God; they will be his people, and God himself will be with them; he will wipe every tear from their eyes. Death will be no more; mourning and crying and pain will be no more, for the first things have passed away.' And the one who was seated on the throne said, 'See, I am making all things new'" (Rev 21:3-5a).

Members of the Lutheran-Roman Catholic Joint Commission

This document was approved unanimously by the members of the Joint Commission, 11 September 1993.

Roman Catholic Members

The Most Rev. Dr. Paul-Werner Scheele (chair from 1988 to 1993)
The Most Rev. Dr. Karl Lehmann (chair from 1986 to 1987)
The Most Rev. Dr. Hans L. Martensen
Prof. Dr. Christian Mhagama
The Most Rev. Dr. Alfons Nossol
Prof. Dr. Vinzenz Pfnür
Prof. Dr. Lothar Ullrich
Prof. Dr. Jared Wicks

Lutheran Members

The Rt. Rev. (retired) Dr. James Crumley (chair)
Prof. Dr. Johannes P. Boendermaker
The Rt. Rev. Dr. Gottfried Brakemeier
The Rt. Rev. Dr. Manas Buthelezi
Prof. Dr. Inge Lönning
Prof. Dr. Dorothea Wendebourg
The Rt. Rev. (emeritus) Dr. Ulrich Wilckens

Consultants

Prof. Dr. Robert Jenson (Lutheran)
Prof. Dr. Aloys Klein (Roman Catholic)
Prof. Dr. Hervé Legrand (Roman Catholic)
Prof. Dr. Harding Meyer (Lutheran)

Staff Members

The Rev. Dr. Eugene L. Brand (Lutheran World Federation)

Msgr. Dr. Basil Meeking (Secretariat for Promoting Christian Unity, 1986 to 1987)

Msgr. Dr. John Radano (Pontifical Council for Promoting Christian Unity)

The Rev. Dr. Heinz-Albert Raem (Pontifical Council for Promoting Christian Unity, from 1990)